P9-DMY-170

DRIVEN

DRIVEN

FROM HOMELESS TO HERO, MY JOURNEYS
ON AND OFF LAMBEAU FIELD

DONALD
DRIVER

WITH PETER GOLENBOCK

CROWN
ARCHETYPE
NEW YORK

Copyright © 2013 by Donald Driver

All rights reserved.
Published in the United States by Crown Archetype,
an imprint of the Crown Publishing Group,
a division of Random House LLC, New York,
a Penguin Random House Company.
www.crownpublishing.com

Crown Archetype with colophon is a trademark of
Random House LLC.

Library of Congress Cataloging-in-Publication Data
Driver, Donald
    Driven: from homeless to hero, my journeys on and
off Lambeau Field/Donald Driver.
        pages cm.
    1. Driver, Donald, 1975. 2. Football players—United
States—Biography. I. Title.
    GV939.D78A3   2013
    796.332092—dc23
    [B]   2013022761

ISBN 978-0-385-34914-7
eISBN 978-0-385-34915-4

Printed in the United States of America

Jacket design by Michael Nagin
Jacket photographs: © Scott McDermott

10 9 8 7 6 5 4 3 2 1

First Edition

To my beautiful wife, Betina,

my son, Cristian,

and my two daughters, Christina and Charity

CONTENTS

DRIVEN

PREFACE

ADVERSITY CAN WRECK your life. Adversity can lay you so low that you never recover. But if you stand up to adversity, it can also make you stronger, wiser, and more compassionate. If you get nothing else out of reading my story, you will come to understand that no matter what your background, no matter what your family life is like, and no matter what obstacles are thrown your way, if you have someone who loves you and looks out for you and if you have a mind to succeed, then anything is possible.

I, Donald Driver, am living proof of that.

For fourteen wonderful years I was a member of the Green Bay Packers football team. I was the teammate of players such as Brett Favre, Desmond Howard, and Aaron Rodgers. After several heartbreaking near misses, painful for me in the retelling, I was blessed to be a member of the 2010 Super Bowl–winning team, and I have to say that earning that ring was one of the highlights of my life. Millions of people watch the Super Bowl on TV, but few truly understand how hard it is to get there and how special it feels to be playing in that game.

In addition to earning that ring, through hard work and a little luck I was able to become the leading receiver in Packers history in catches with 743 and yards gained with 10,137.

The luck was staying away from serious injury, as I was able to play in 205 games, second-most in Packer history after Brett Favre.

I also had the privilege of participating in the reality show *Dancing with the Stars*. I became the third NFL football player to win the contest and the Mirror Bowl, which meant almost as much to me as winning the Super Bowl. The preparation was grueling, as you will see.

It's been quite a ride.

Looking back I would constantly ask myself, *How did this African American kid growing up on the mean streets of Houston do it?*

The answer lies between the covers of this book.

As a teenager I had little stability as my family moved from place to place. When things got really bad we lived in a U-Haul under a bridge for several months, cooking meals on a hibachi. Father figures drifted in and out of my life, and I had a mom who worked at night, leaving my brother and me to our own devices.

The way I started out in life, dealing drugs and stealing cars, it's quite possible that if events had occurred differently, I could have ended up in jail, or worse, six feet under. When I decided to write this book, I did it because I wanted people—especially young people—to know that we all make mistakes in life and, more important, we can overcome them.

I was fortunate. Unlike many of my relatives and friends who grew up with me in Houston's ghetto, I had a talent I could use to escape my hardscrabble, street-kid youth. I had a mother who loved me and grandparents who supported me, and after I left Houston to go to college, I met a woman who helped me to find a more righteous path in life. Thanks to my wife, Tina, I became successful and right-minded.

You know of my toughness and my smile. Now you'll know why I pick up after myself in hotel rooms, why my mother is a hero, and why my wife is my strength. You'll know why I make my family wear seat belts, and why I am devoted to the Packers fans who always believed in me.

I am proud of the receptions and the touchdowns, but I am prouder of the family I am raising and the charity work I do. I am most proud of being a doting husband and a proud papa.

This is my real story. It isn't a story invented to make me look good. I've decided to let you readers come with me every step of the way on my journey of life—smiling through it all.

CHAPTER 1

CHILD
OF THE
HOOD

My dad, Marvin Driver Jr., it has been said to me many times, was one of the best quarterbacks ever to come out of Texas high school football. He was the starting quarterback his freshman year at Drew High School in Crosby, Texas, a town about thirty-five miles northeast of Houston. My dad could throw the ball seventy-eight yards in the air. The legend is that he kicked a football from a tee from one end zone to the other barefoot in the winter. I suspect that was how he earned the nickname "Steel-Toe."

Time brought change to Texas. After *Brown v. Board of Education*, integration became mandatory, and race relations in the South turned really ugly. Drew High School, where my mom as well as dad went to school, was all black, and Crosby High School was all white. When the courts ordered the integration of Crosby High, the whites rioted.

At that point all the black players decided they didn't want to play with the white boys, and they quit the team—all except my dad, whose father told him, "We're not quitters. We're going to fight this, and you're going to play football."

Dad said he was stunned by what happened next: Most of the hatred toward him came not from the whites but from people of his own race. He was called "whitey lover," and one day he opened up his locker and was horrified to see a

9

stuffed monkey hanging with a rope around its neck with a sign that said, "Quit nigger or you'll wish you had."

My dad, scared, went home and told his father what happened.

"Stay strong," his father advised him.

My dad stayed on the football team, even though the white coaches made him backup behind a less talented white quarterback.

Sports often is an antidote to prejudice and racism. Coaches and fans want to win, and, even in the 1960s, if the white guy couldn't do the job, to save his own job a white coach would put in the more talented black player. Once a player can help a coach win, the color of the player's skin no longer matters.

The Crosby Cougars football team wasn't doing very well under their white quarterback, and so as a last resort the coach put my dad in, and my dad brought the team victories.

As my father tells the story, the crowd would yell, "We want Driver! We want Driver!"

He told me, "It gave everyone, including me, goose bumps."

(To show how times have changed, I never once—not in high school or in college—felt the sting of racism.)

My dad became the captain of the Crosby Cougars, and he was recruited and given a scholarship to Texas A&M, but he never went because life threw him for a big loss when his father died unexpectedly his senior year.

My father was the eldest of ten children, and he felt the pressure of suddenly having to be the breadwinner of the family. With his father's income gone, his mother, Betty, had to raise ten children by herself. Money was very hard to come by.

Before his dad died, my father had had big dreams. He saw himself as an NFL quarterback. He loved *Perry Mason,* his favorite TV show, and he fancied himself becoming a lawyer. But with the death of his father, his dreams died with him. When he graduated from Crosby High School in June 1971, he married his girlfriend, Faye—my mother—and went to work. He drove a truck during the day, and he had a second job working in a canning factory in Highlands, Texas, as a machine operator.

People who saw him play still talk about him, bragging about how he was such a great quarterback and how he could have made it to the pros. And it's tough, because it's forty years later and he still thinks about that. When I got older, my dad would pull out the old 8 mm films and show us how he could throw and run, how he would jump off a blocker's back and run down the sideline. There he was captured on film, the captain of the football team and the school homecoming king standing alongside my mother, the homecoming queen and the head cheerleader.

He met Faye in high school. She was a little country girl who lived on a farm. She was beautiful, smart, and had a great sense of humor. Mom was hardworking, independent, and very loving. She was twenty-one years old when she had my sister Tamela; was twenty-two when she had Marvin; and twenty-three when she had me, so she was pretty young. What I remember most about her when I was a child was that she was very affectionate. We were always hugging, always kissing. My mom would greet me with "Hey baby," and she'd wrap her arms around me and plant a big kiss on me. Today mom is sixty, but she never changed. She's still that same loving, passionate person.

My given name was Donald, but no one ever called me that. My nickname was Quickie. Everyone called me Quickie Driver, never Donald. As an infant my mom had called me Quickie because I was so fast she had a lot of trouble catching me when she went to put a diaper on me. My dad said that every time I got in trouble and he wanted to spank me, I'd take off running. He said he rarely could catch me.

In the end my father couldn't get over his not fulfilling his dreams in football. Time went on, and the fame and the stardom became more and more distant. After high school, the way my father tells it, he met new friends. Jobs were scarce for African Americans, and he and his new friends were desperate to provide for their families. You don't have a lot of choices when finding a job isn't possible. He and his new friends sold drugs. They robbed and stole. When my mom was pregnant with me in May 1974, my dad went to prison for robbing a convenience store.

Dad was locked up for six months—he insisted he was innocent, but as with many defendants, he worried about what a jury would do and pleaded guilty in exchange for a shorter prison sentence. He figured it was better than having the case go to trial, losing, and serving a much longer sentence.

"When I got out," my dad told me, "I did didn't take my eight-year probation sentence seriously."

He got in trouble again, this time for drug possession, and with that came a new arrest warrant. He was sent back to jail, this time for two years, although it was reduced to eight months and twenty-four days. After he got out of jail, he was caught with a pistol and had to return once again.

The truth is, I had no father figure when I was young. My dad wasn't around when I was born, and with him in and out of jail, my mom decided to part ways with him when I was two years old. She had three children and didn't want us growing up with a part-time father. She set out for a new life. My mother took us to Baton Rouge, Louisiana, and didn't tell my father where we moved. I didn't know that at the time.

For years dad had no way of tracking us down, until he hired a private detective, who determined where we were living. Once he found her, he pleaded with her to come back to Houston.

Because of these trials, I didn't meet my father until I was six years old. I remember it like it was yesterday. My mom drove to my paternal grandparents' house in the Hattiesburg section of Houston in her green Oldsmobile Cutlass Supreme. My dad had just gotten out of prison, and he was inside my grandparents' home waiting for us.

Inside I met a tall, smiling stranger who had this whole goatee thing going on.

"Quickie," my mom said to me, "this is your dad."

He looked like a tough guy.

I was caught by surprise. I looked at him like, *Who is that? I don't know that guy. Who are you?*

After my mom and siblings moved to Houston, the relationship between my parents cooled, and we saw little of my father.

• • •

MY MOTHER THEN fell in love with a man named Sam Gray, and after they got married, Sam became my father. Officially he was my stepdad, of course, but I was young, and to me he wasn't anything but my dad.

The years I lived with mom and Sam were among the better ones of my childhood. Sam was everything you would want in a father. While living in Baton Rouge, my mother had had a boyfriend, and she gave birth to a fourth child, a beautiful baby girl named Patrice. Sam took us all in and raised us as if we were his own. Sam's no longer with us, and I get teary-eyed and choked up just talking about him. Sam, who didn't have any kids of his own, raised us during my formative years. He didn't have to do it, but he did. Sam fell in love with my mother, and he fell in love with us. He was great, and I loved him to death.

From Sam, I learned that anyone can father a child, but not everyone can be a father to a child. By the time I was in the second grade, Sam and I were connected. He'd always do things for us. He never hesitated. Sam was always there for us.

It's hard to find a good man like that.

When my mom was married to Sam, they had a baby, Sam Jr. I had a little sister, Patrice, but I didn't have a little brother, so when Sam Jr. came along I thought that was great. My older brother Marvin wasn't so sure.

"I have one little brother. That's enough," he said. But once Sam Jr. was old enough to walk and talk, he was thrilled to have a little brother he could pick on. We loved to tease him, but we were also his bodyguards. We protected him. We were always there for him.

Sam's job was driving a bus for handicapped people to and from MD Anderson Hospital in Houston. Short and chubby, he had hair on the sides and was bald in the middle. He reminded me of George Jefferson.

Every Tuesday night Sam went out bowling and brought home all these bowling trophies. Usually we would go with him because that's what the family did. And I can still bowl pretty well because of him.

When it was homework time, Sam would walk through the door and yell, "Hey, it's time, let's get your homework done!"

Sam was always supportive, and when we did wrong, mom gave him the right to spank us. Sam was our dad; that's how we looked at him.

When we were with Sam, we had stability. We lived in a nice middle-class home. Sam had a job and my mother worked cleaning hotel rooms.

For years she had worked as a housekeeper from morning until evening. When we were very young she would take us with her to work. She wasn't supposed to have us there. She'd say to me, "Don't move from this spot. Stay here." And I would stay and wait until she came back.

As I got older, I would go into the rooms with her, and I'd watch her work. I saw the way people would abuse hotel rooms—it was terrible.

I saw how hard my mom worked to get those rooms cleaned. Maybe that's why, to this day, when I leave a hotel room, I always try to clean up. For me I find it tough to leave a hotel room with wet towels thrown all over the place. I just can't do it. I take them up and put them in a pile. I always pick up the trash and throw it in the wastebasket.

Around the time I was in fifth grade, my mom went back to school to get a license to be a security guard.

"I don't want to just clean hotel rooms for a living for the rest of my life," she said. "I need to do something better."

My mother's determination to improve her lot sparked something in me. I can never forget seeing this woman determined to make a better life for herself.

ONE QUIRKY THING about my mom: She had the traveler's blues. For some reason she didn't like to stay in one spot. She felt like she needed to keep moving—as a child you don't really question these things, but it was unsettling.

She wasn't running from bill collectors. She always paid her bills on time.

We moved rather frequently, and we would change schools each time we moved. Maybe she thought she was improving herself with each move. I don't know. I do know it wasn't good for her kids.

Why are we moving again? we would constantly ask ourselves.

Sam liked to be settled, and moving drove him crazy. We were never in one place long enough to enjoy it. I would be at one elementary school, we'd up and move, and I'd go to another elementary school. And then another. And another.

I attended a different elementary school each year from kindergarten to fifth grade. It was as though my mother was running from something, but we never knew from what. The reasons my mom gave for picking up stakes usually had to do with an issue at the school we were attending. Either one of us kids was getting in trouble, or we didn't like the teachers, or we didn't like the other kids. Someone was always getting into fights. Among my brother Moses, my sister Tamela, and me, something was always wrong in her mind.

We would also get into it with our neighbors. We had our normal kids accidents, too, of course, which probably terrified mom.

When Mom was married to Sam we lived in several middle-class areas of Houston. We lived in South Park, Martin Luther King, and in an apartment off MacGregor Way, where one afternoon Moses was hit by a car. We were playing tag, and he ran into the middle of the street. A car hit him and flipped him over and broke his leg. When he came back from the hospital, he had a cast on his leg from thigh to ankle.

Mom decided it was time to move.

Eventually her need to move took a terrible toll. When I was in the fifth grade mom wanted to move yet again. My brother Moses was in the sixth grade, and a kid was picking on him. He would get in a fight every day, and he didn't want to go to that school anymore. But to go to another school, he would have to get on a bus and travel a long way to get there. My mother decided that rather than put Moses on a bus, we'd move again.

Sam finally put his foot down.

"Faye, I'm not moving anymore," he said. "I can't keep doing this. You have to understand. This is it. Stay. Let's not keep moving because you're not comfortable or happy."

My mother gave him an ultimatum.

"If you don't want to move," she said, "I'm moving without you."

And she moved with her kids, leaving Sam behind.

Only as time went on, and her kids got older and split up, did she realize that staying in one place would have been better than the constant moving, especially after we moved into bad neighborhoods.

Without Sam, our father.

MOM NO LONGER had Sam's income, and so she moved into the Fifth Ward of Houston, an old, secluded area with private homes but mostly Section 8 apartments and low-income housing. You might say we were living in Houston's ghetto. The residents were African American and Cuban, and the unemployment rate there was probably 60 percent. Where we lived no one drove a nice car and headed off to work. No one had a comfort zone. Everything was a struggle.

Mom was working as a security guard from 11 P.M. to 7 A.M. She'd go to work and leave behind five children. Tamela was in the eighth grade, Moses seventh, and I was in the sixth. Little sister Patrice was in the second grade, and Sam Jr. was just a toddler. As the older ones, we were in charge of watching and taking care of the younger ones.

Before Mom would leave for work, she would ask our

next-door neighbor, J.R., "Would you please keep an eye on the kids for me?

J.R. was tall, about six foot five, and he had to be in his early twenties.

"Momma, I got them," he would always say. "Go ahead and go to work."

J.R. would take care of us all right. If we needed something from the store he would run there, get it, and bring it back. During the three years we lived there—it was about the only time Mom didn't pick up and move after a year—J.R. became the bond, the father figure my brother, sister, and I didn't have. We looked up to him. What Mom never knew was that J.R. was a big-time drug dealer, and it wasn't long before Moses and I went to work for him.

When Tamela turned thirteen, she met a boy in the neighborhood and started hanging out with him at night. The young children, Trice and Sam, would be asleep by the time Mom left for work at ten thirty, and that gave Moses and me the opportunity to sneak out after she left.

We lived in a dangerous neighborhood, and my brother and I realized that if we didn't become part of the drug scene, we would be outcasts. We wanted to be part of the dominant culture because this was what most of my extended family was doing. My father, my uncles, and many of our friends were dealing drugs—and we wanted to fit in.

J.R. offered Moses and me fifty dollars each a night to stand on the street and watch for the police while he was making his drug deals. If a police car came, we'd yell or make enough noise to give the drug dealers the heads-up to take off. Every night we had a different signal. One night it was "Blue, blue"; another night it was "one time." I'd say "blue, blue" and I'd hear someone else scream "blue, blue" and everyone would just start running. The police would scatter through the neighborhood looking for suspects, but they always came up empty.

"What are you guys doing outside?" the cops would ask me.

I was never scared. I felt invincible. I knew they didn't have anything on me. All I was doing was yelling something. I was bold enough as a kid to talk back.

"I can be outside," I'd answer. "What are *you* doing here?"

Sometimes the police would search us.

"I didn't do anything," I'd keep repeating, because I hadn't.

The cops would check my background. I had no warrants and no run-ins, and they would have to let me go.

"Go home!" they would yell at me and my friends.

"Nope," I'd say. "I'm not going home. I don't have to."

I would sit back down on the corner where they found me. That was my attitude then.

No one lived a normal life in the Fifth Ward. Normal for me was walking down the street at one in the morning and staying out all night.

The hundred dollars a night Moses and I took in was big money in 1987, but my mom never knew. We would break the hundred into smaller bills, and every once in a while we'd slip some money into her purse. She paid the rent with the checks from her job, but it didn't go much further, and if I saw she was having trouble with the light bill, say, I'd always make sure she had the money to pay it. She'd go through her purse, and she'd find the money, and she'd say, "Shoot, I had it after all."

Having money made me feel important. Having money made me feel a heck of a lot better than when I was dirt poor. Moses and I were able to buy expensive shoes. We, like every other kid in the country, wanted Nike Jordans. My sister's boyfriend, who was also a drug dealer, preferred Fila athletic wear, and so we used to call him Fila-man. He wore Fila clothes from head to foot. Tamela fell in love with him and had four kids with him. They were together all through my high school and college days, and then they drifted apart.

Moses and I made enough money working for J.R. that we were able to became established drug dealers ourselves. We'd give him five hundred dollars and he'd give us a decent supply of drugs, and we'd make $1,200 selling it to the people in the hood.

Most of the guys who sold drugs sold marijuana. One reason they did it was that the penalty was much less if they got caught. But to me selling marijuana seemed too difficult because it wasn't a big attraction in my neighborhood. Most of the people I knew who did drugs wanted something other than pot. Besides, weed was just too much work. After you bought it, you had to break it up, get rid of the seeds, and put it in bags. Other drugs were a lot easier and much more profitable.

It was a fast life. What saved me from going to prison was that though I sold drugs, I never used them. I never used them because I saw what they did to other people. I saw how they really transformed people's lives, people who went from a nice, comfortable middle-class life to pawning or selling a microwave

21

or stealing jewelry from their family, or taking money from a mother's purse. I saw how they took over people's lives, and always for the worse. So I knew what drugs could get you.

The other thing was, if you used drugs, that took away from your money supply, because now you were addicted to what you were selling. I never wanted to do that. There was nothing positive about using drugs.

The big-time drug dealers I knew didn't use drugs, either. They realized they were a product to make them money. If they took drugs, they knew they'd just be strung-out junkies like their buyers.

I never thought about how selling drugs might jeopardize someone's life. Back then, when I was struggling to help my mother so we could pay the bills, I didn't care who I hurt. I had family members who became addicted to cocaine. If it was the neighbor down the street or a family member, I didn't care. When I look back, I feel terribly guilty that I was selling drugs.

I don't know why, but I never feared getting caught. As a kid I had no choice but to grow up fast. Maybe if I had grown up like a normal kid with normal parents and a normal upbringing, it all would have been different.

I also had no fear of dying. I can't tell you how many times I looked down the barrel of a gun. It happened so many times. The first time I was in the seventh grade in middle school. Moses was in the eighth grade. We were working for J.R.

I was sitting on the curb bouncing a tennis ball. The tennis ball was filled with drugs. If you make a small cut in a tennis ball, you can pop it open and drop your drugs into it.

If you don't make the hole too big, the ball closes up and still bounces.

I often would sit there bouncing the tennis ball, and one night a good friend of mine named Corey came by with four of his friends. Corey lived in a different apartment complex, but we knew each other from school. I didn't know his friends from Adam and Eve, but I knew Corey. He came up to me and started talking.

"What's up, Quick?" he asked. "What's going on?"

"Nothing, man," I said. "Just hanging on the curb. It's what we do."

One of the other guys kept saying, "What do you got?"

"Who are you?" I asked him.

We were bantering back and forth when my boy Corey pulled a pistol on me.

I thought he was joking. I knocked the gun away from my face.

"What are you doing?" I asked him.

He took a step back and leveled the gun at my face again. He was nervous and shaking.

"Corey, what are you pulling a gun on me for?" I asked.

"Man, where's the drugs?"

He knew they were in the tennis ball, which I threw down the street as far as I could.

"They're in the tennis ball!" Corey yelled at the other guys.

I wanted to fight them, but I realized I was outnumbered. It was one against five, and fighting them wasn't going to work.

As Corey and his four friends started after the ball, my

brother Moses came around the corner, and when they saw him, they started running. Moses and I chased them, and we caught one of them and beat him real bad.

They took the ball with the drugs in it, and I lost a lot of money. Now I had to figure out how to get it back. You have to go back out onto the streets and hustle again.

Corey and I no longer were friends. In fact, I never saw him again.

THE DRUG RUNNERS for J.R. had nicknames. I never knew any of their real names. One afternoon a friend by the name of Red lent my brother Moses his little Mustang in exchange for some drugs. Moses was thirteen. I was twelve.

"Be careful," Red said.

Moses wasn't old enough to have a license, and I had never driven before.

My brother drove down a back road.

"It's time you got behind the wheel," he said.

"No," I said. "Red is going to kill us."

"You'll be fine," Moses said. "Red won't be mad at us."

At age twelve I was tall enough to reach the gas pedal and brake and see over the windshield. I drove Red's car around town until I felt comfortable driving.

"Next thing we've got to learn to do," I said, "is steal cars."

Stealing cars attracted me because of the adrenaline rush. It was something to look forward to. You were going to run from the police and make a nice score. At the time, that was what I considered fun. There were also times when I'd steal a car and then use it to pick up girls and drive around. It was all about show.

Stealing cars, it turned out, was just as easy as selling drugs. The easiest cars to steal were those old Cadillacs. I'd stake out the streets of Houston, a T-shirt wrapped around my right fist. I would punch out the back window, and in a flash I'd be inside. Within thirty seconds I'd be ready to roll.

I learned from cousins and an uncle who were experts in these things that hot-wiring a car took too much time. They taught me it was much quicker to take a screwdriver, break the steering wheel so it could move, and then stick the screwdriver into the hole for the key to the ignition and turn it, and it would pop. Once it popped, I could start the car.

Usually I'd steal the car for parts. I'd drive it to the warehouse and drop it off, and the men at the chop shop would break it apart. They paid for the whole car, not each piece. If you pulled up in a Mercedes, they'd look at you and say, "Nice car," and hand you a grand or five hundred dollars. You took the money and got out of there, because you didn't want to be around if the cops ever showed up.

I would steal cars at gas stations.

One time I was riding in a car with a friend, and another driver cut him off. My friend blew his horn and the driver gave us the finger.

"Follow him," I said. "I'm going to teach him a lesson."

We trailed him at a safe distance as he pulled into a gas station to buy something in its store: cigarettes, candy, or a lottery ticket. When he closed the driver's side door and walked inside I didn't hear the telltale beep–beep that you get when the driver locks the car, and I saw that the tailpipe was still puffing smoke. The car was running and the key was still in it. You'd be surprised how many people do that when they bop quickly in to buy something at a gas station or a convenience store.

I jogged to his car—a Honda Accord with expensive rims—jumped inside, slammed the door, blew the horn, and waited for him to come out. When he saw me, I gave him the finger and sped off. He was lucky I didn't take his car to sell it. I just took it to piss him off. I drove it about six blocks and left it in a Walmart parking lot as if to say, *You cut us off. Don't be a jerk.*

My friend thought I was absolutely nuts.

I stole perhaps thirty cars. I was very good at selecting the right cars to steal and I was a skilled driver. I only had to escape from the police once. Just as I was starting the car, I heard sirens. I floored it, and I was flying along, checking the mirror to see how close the police were. I drove into a back alley and slowed to about twenty miles an hour. When an older woman backed her car out of her driveway into my path, I T-boned her car. I jumped out and took off running.

I had about a block head start on the cops, but I was concerned about the woman, so I circled back to see if she was all right. The police were around the corner.

"Go sit on my porch," the woman said.

I trusted her. Exactly why, I'm not sure. When the police questioned her, she said the driver had run off.

"Who is that on your porch swing?" she was asked.

"Oh, that's my grandson," she said.

After the police left, the woman ordered me into her house.

"Why did you do this, young man?" she wanted to know. "You could be doing so much more with your life."

Her name was Evelyn Johnson, and I never forgot her kindness. We would become close. After she did that for me, I felt as though she were a guardian angel watching over me. In truth her kindness didn't change my mind about how I was going to live my life—I continued to sell drugs and steal cars. She would warn me what might happen, but her words went in one ear and came out the other. Even so, I knew I owed her everything because she gave the opportunity to continue to live my life. If it weren't for Miss Johnson, I know I'd have ended up doing a couple of years in juvenile detention.

Miss Johnson was a great Christian woman. She believed that God allows people to get second chances in life.

"You have your whole life ahead of you," she said to me. "You're so young. This is your second chance in life right now."

"Thank you," I said when I walked out of her house, then went back to my way of life, always looking over my shoulder for the cops.

Still, Miss Johnson was always there when I needed her. I would go over to her house just to say hello. If she needed something from the grocery store or if she needed me to pick something up, I was always there for her. I felt I owed her that. I felt I owed her my life because that day she had given me the chance to get it back.

She was like having a second grandmother, which is what I needed, someone who was always going to try to keep me straight.

"How are you doing? How are your grades?" she would say to me.

It was what I needed. My biological grandmother was saying it, but it's always great to hear it from someone else, too. She would want to know all about the positive things I was doing. Later, when I was invited to try out for the Olympics, she was excited. It put a smile on my face knowing I had made her happy.

When I was in college I would call her and ask how she was feeling. Whenever I visited Houston, I would go back and see her. In time she got sick, and during my sophomore year in college she passed away.

Whenever I think about Miss Johnson, and her kindness and her ability to forgive, I miss her.

Despite going to bed many a time at four in the morning after a night of dealing and stealing, I somehow got enough sleep to go to school and to do well. I was a smart kid and a B student. Despite my drug dealing, I never did anything to jeopardize my advancing to the next grade. I knew education was important, though I wanted to be in the streets because that's where the money was.

Growing up where I did in the projects of Houston, all I saw were drug dealers and drugs. I saw people who were on crack. It was so prevalent that as a kid you thought this was the way life was supposed to be. As an impressionable middle schooler I told myself, *If I wanted to make any sort of decent money, this was the way it had to be.*

There were certainly more legitimate ways to make money than drug dealing or car stealing, but there wasn't enough money in it. It wasn't about getting a job at McDonald's or working at a plant for minimum wage. I wanted cars, jewelry, and Air Jordans, and the only way I was going to get them was by selling drugs.

It was a lifestyle I was accustomed to. It was the way of life. It was how I grew up, living around people who sold drugs, people who stole cars. I had uncles and cousins in the drug business. One uncle was making a great living selling drugs, driving his Mercedes-Benz to the house he owned. I would ask him for money, and he'd peel off a twenty and give it to me. It seemed easy for him. So that's what I thought I had to do.

As I got older, I thought about breaking tradition, but my family was heavy into dealing drugs and stealing cars, so I figured I should do that, too.

I DIDN'T THINK much about the consequences of getting caught because at age thirteen, I knew the system well enough to know that if I got caught, all they were going to do was send me to a juvenile detention center. At juvie you didn't do hard time. You didn't go behind the big steel bars. You had a room and a roommate; you had decent meals. You think, *Okay, if I have to do this for two or three years, who cares? I'm fine with it.* We knew nothing bad was going to come of it. In fact, for a lot of kids, it was a far better environment than where they were coming from.

And so as I began my teen years in middle school I led a double life. In the daytime I was a student. At night I was a drug dealer and car thief. Mom would walk into our apartment after a night's work as a security guard at 7:30 A.M., and Moses and I would be sleeping on the living room floor.

"Hey, get up, let's go!" Mom would yell, and we'd get up and she'd drive us to school. She'd drop us off, then go home and sleep.

At school I was the quiet guy, everyone's friend, and the jokester. I wanted to be liked by everyone. I wanted to be popular, and I was, even with the teachers.

"Quickie! Stop joking around," the teachers were always saying. But I was also the teacher's pet, even though I knew some of the wiseguy kids frowned on that. I wanted to build that good-kid reputation for myself, and I wasn't afraid of bullies. My attitude was *I'm not afraid of anyone or anything.*

AFTER WE MOVED away from Sam, my mom and my biological dad started dating again.

This is the opportunity for them to get back together, I remember thinking. What every kid in that situation wishes for. *Mom and Dad are getting back together. This is awesome.*

In my mind all I saw were lollipops and roses, but it turned out to be a disaster. One night my mom was supposed to meet my dad at this club. She got there and . . . he was with someone else.

He came over to the apartment and my mom screamed

at him to get out. My brother and I were in bed in our room, and I could hear them fighting.

My dad walked in, gave us a kiss, and said, "Y'all be good. I'm gone."

My father walked out of the door, and that was it between them. At the time, Mom didn't tell us what happened. We only found out after Mom got mad at me for sticking up for my dad.

"You think your dad is such an angel," she said. "Your dad hit me."

"What do you mean, he hit you?" I asked.

Not long afterward I confronted my dad. He didn't deny it.

"I wish you'd hit her one more time," I said, staring as menacingly as I could into his face.

"Are you threatening me?" he asked.

"I promise this is no threat," I said. "If you ever put your hands on Mom again, I will kill you."

Dad wasn't the person to let a threat like that go unchallenged.

"Before I let you put your hands on me," he said, "I'll put you six feet under."

It was a standoff, but it was a turning point for me and my dad for a long time. The night when my father went out the door was the last time my mom ever thought about getting back together with him. And she never looked back.

Unfortunately, that's when she met Tom.

CHAPTER 2

HOMELESS

WE HIT IT OFF—in the beginning. Tom Williams was The Man. He was tall, dark-skinned, with little beady eyes. And he had a good head of hair and full beard. My mom was in her thirties, and Tom was in his mid-thirties, when my mom fell head over heels in love with him. And for a while, so did we.

Tom was a sugar daddy. He was everything my mom wanted. He came in flashy; he left flashy.

The first time Mom introduced him to us kids, Tom had a briefcase and wore a suit. I was eleven years old, in the sixth grade. We were living in the projects down the hall from J.R. I was making enough money from selling drugs and stealing cars that I really didn't mind where we were living. I would have enjoyed a more middle-class existence, but I was getting along very well on my own, and I wasn't complaining. I rarely saw my mom, who was working nights, but I had enough friends from the projects and the street to keep me company and fill my time.

When we met Tom, he told us he was a lawyer. Mom and he dated for almost two years, and often he would stay overnight at our apartment. When he did he would get up in the morning, put on his suit, grab his briefcase, walk out the door, and leave as though he were going to work.

"I'm going to the office," he would say. And he'd drive off in his car.

Moses and I were sure Mom had hit the jackpot.

Mom is dating a lawyer. This is great!

Or so we thought.

"Faye, you won't have to work anymore," Tom would say to her. He'd tell us, "I'm going to take care of you guys. You guys don't have to do anything but be with me."

Wow, Mom, we're going to be good, we thought. *We're finally going to be okay. We're going to be taken care of.*

Or so we thought.

Then for three straight days Tom stayed home.

Before my mom left for her job, she'd ask him, "Aren't you going to work today?"

"No, I don't have anything to do today," he said.

We figured he didn't have a legal case to work on.

"Okay," she said, and off she went.

After a while Tom began to just stay home. I wondered whether Tom had been lying to us about his being a lawyer. It didn't matter. Mom loved him, and love is blind.

During the whole time they dated I always wondered why we never went to his place.

"Oh, he lives far away," Mom would say, or she would cover for him in some other way.

The proof he was a con artist came when it was time to renew our apartment lease. He told Mom to let it lapse because he was buying us a house.

"Hey, I got a new place, in Humble, Texas," he said. "I'm

buying a house, and it's beautiful. I'm just waiting to close on it, and I'll sign the paperwork, and we'll move in."

It all sounded too good to be true.

We rented a U-Haul truck and packed up our things from the apartment. We drove from Houston to Humble, Texas, a small town with oil refineries located just north of Houston near the international airport.

We five children rode in the back of the U-Haul truck while Mom sat in front with Tom. For us it was an exciting adventure. We couldn't wait to see where we were going. *A house!?* I couldn't even picture it.

Tom stopped the truck. Mom opened the back, and we rushed out to look at the house. In front of us was a big, beautiful brick house with a spacious yard for us to play. I was elated.

Yes, this is it! I thought.

I had been hoping for a middle-class neighborhood, but this was even ritzier than that. This was the high end, where the richest of the rich lived.

Wow!

All the other houses in the neighborhood were equally amazing.

This is so beautiful; Mom struck it rich, I thought.

The euphoria didn't last long.

"The key is in the mailbox," he said.

Tom went up to the house.

There was no key.

He looked under the mat.

There was no key.

"I have to run up to the gas station to make a phone call," he said. "A woman's going to meet us here in a few minutes."

We waited. No woman came.

That's when I started to become suspicious.

Are we moving in or what? I wondered.

"They won't call me back," Tom kept saying.

I couldn't figure out what had gone wrong. Had Tom made the whole thing up, and if he had, why did he go to the trouble, knowing it wasn't going to work out in the end. To this day I don't know what sort of con Tom was pulling, whether some sort of arrangement had fallen through or whether he had made the whole thing up. Either way, it never made any sense.

We had left the apartment, handed in the keys, and here we were on the road in a strange neighborhood with no place to go.

Mom and Tom started to get into it.

"What are we going to do, Tom?" Mom wanted to know. "Where are the kids going to sleep?"

We got back in the U-Haul and drove to my mom's parents' house in Crosby, Texas. Stella Brock, my mom's mother, told her, "Baby, come on home."

But my mom's father wasn't having any of it. He wasn't fooled by Tom's briefcase, suit, or his big talk. He told her she and the children could stay, but she couldn't bring Tom.

"I don't care for men who won't take care of my daughter," he said.

My mom refused to leave Tom and was indignant at the rebuff of him. We drove away in a huff.

That night we slept under a tall bridge in our U-Haul truck. We pulled out the pots and pans, lit a fire, and cooked canned Vienna sausages and patties. That night we slept in the back of the truck.

Mom tried to find a place for us to stay, but it wasn't easy considering Tom had told her she could quit her job, and she had. She didn't have money for the security deposit. Tom, it turned out, was himself broke and unemployed.

Days went by. Tom did nothing. Homeless, we lived under that bridge for about a month. Mom would cash her food stamps, and every once in a while we'd spend a night in a motel. When her money ran out, we'd go back under the bridge. Sometimes she allowed us kids to go stay with our grandparents while she and Tom stayed together in the truck.

During the day we would drive to our grandparents' house or to the home of a friend of my mom's and take showers and change clothes. Then we'd go back and sleep in the U-Haul.

My mom finally decided to accept her parents' offer with the conditions that her father gave her; her kids went to stay with them but Tom—and my mom—did not. We stayed with my grandparents for a couple of weeks until my mother's retirement check arrived and she had money again.

"Hey, let's go."

My mom found an apartment she could afford in Baytown, Texas, twenty miles east of Houston and only fifteen minutes from Crosby. Mom was able to furnish the new place because in addition to her retirement check, she had just gotten her tax refund. She even bought Moses and me a new water bed. It was awesome for us. We thought it was amazing.

This is perfect. Or so we thought.

And then one day after Moses and I came home from school, we saw a big lock on the door, and we couldn't get in. I peeked inside. Most of our belongings were gone. The marshals had come and had cleaned the place out. To get in we had to break a window and climb inside.

I didn't know it, but we had been months behind on our rent, and a collection agency came and took almost everything. We spent the night in the empty apartment, found what clothing was left, and the next day we loaded up Mom's car and went to school. The other kids in my class had no idea what I was going through. That I could function at all with such chaos happening all around me was amazing.

Moses and I knew it was over for us. I knew we had hit the bottom. After spending two years with Tom, this was how we had ended up.

I remember it all vividly, but above all I remember that I had to grow up very fast. I don't ever remember being a kid. I don't remember just being in the backyard playing with my friends. What I remember most about my childhood was always having to pack up and leave, stay a short time, and pack up and leave again. Time and time again.

My mom and Tom were trying to figure things out, where to go and what to do next. My mom decided that she wanted me, Moses, little brother Sam Jr., and Trice to stay with Sam, my stepdad. Even though my mom was still dating Tom, Sam must have taken pity on us and agreed. I suspect that Sam also was still in love with my mom.

Tom waited in the car while Mom and Sam talked. We settled in, thinking this was where we would be staying the night. Moses and I were in our nightclothes in the next room, listening to Mom and Sam argue and fuss.

"Sam, I'm not staying," I could hear Mom say. "I'm going. Let the kids stay the night, Sam. They have nowhere to sleep, and I'll be back in the morning."

Sam wanted her back. He begged her.

"Faye, Faye, Faye. Let's talk about it," he pleaded.

But Mom wouldn't have it. She was in love with slimeball Tom. Looking back on it now, I think Sam was trying to protect my mom and probably us, too, from Tom.

Moses and I stood there as Mom and Sam argued. Sam grabbed Mom, and Mom swung her hand and tried to hit him. When Sam swung back, Moses and I rushed in and grabbed him. Sam was small, and I picked him up and held him up off the floor against the wall. I don't know where the strength came from—I was barely a teenager.

In slow, loud words I told him, "If you *ever* in your life lift a finger to my mom again, I promise you, I will kill you."

My brother was behind me, saying the same thing.

"Get your stuff," my mother ordered us. I told Moses to get my things while I held Sam, protecting Mom. We left. From that point on, our relationship with Sam was over.

Before we left, Sam insisted that Mom leave behind Sam Jr., who was two. He threatened to call the police if she didn't. We didn't have a place to live, and Sam didn't want his son living in a U-Haul truck. Mom left Sam Jr. with Sam because she was afraid that if the authorities were called, they would take away all five of her kids, and she would have been destroyed if they had done that.

Sam Jr. grew up with his dad and another child Sam had, a girl I didn't know. My little brother Sam never did understand why we left him behind that night.

"We didn't want to leave you—but your dad wouldn't let you go," we told him many years later.

Leaving Sam Jr. was tough. It was really, really tough.

That night we stayed at Tom's parents' house in Kashmere Gardens, near the Fifth Ward of Houston, and we stayed with them for a couple of months.

So much happened in this year of my life. It was like there's point A and you want to get to point B, but you never get there because there are so many obstacles in the way. I think back to every place I lived as a kid—I lived all over the city of Houston. We moved around so much then that I used to christen every new home by jumping off the roof. My thinking was if I didn't break my leg it was a good place to live. What a crazy kid I was. I thought I was Superman or Spider-Man. I thought that I could fly.

I never got hurt. I was lucky.

WHEN MOM AND Sam separated and Sam kept Sam Jr. with him, that was the turning point. We had lost little Sam. He didn't grow up with us and Mom, and that's what we missed more than anything. We missed the bond we had, always

being there for him as his protectors, all of us loving and supporting one another.

It was tough for all of us, and then because of Tom, the family broke up further when my sister Tamela, who was fourteen,
went to live with my dad, Marvin Driver. With little Sam gone,
Moses, my little sister Trice, and I were left to live with Mom
and Tom in substandard housing in the projects of Houston.

It was tough not having all the pieces together. We had
called ourselves the Little Brady Bunch, but after the family
broke up we struggled with the separation. It's why we're so
close today as adults, because of the journey we had to take.
It's truly been a blessing, because the ordeal brought us closer
and closer together as a family as we got older.

AWAY FROM J.R. and in a strange neighborhood, I wasn't
making any drug money at the time. We were impoverished.
We had very little furniture. We'd sleep on the floor, or we
lay on a mattress on the floor and slept. We didn't have a
couch or a TV. We didn't even have an iron to press our
clothes. We used to put our clothes under the mattress on
the floor and lie on them to press them so we'd look nice
going to school in the morning.

For the time being this was home. The water was working and so was the gas, and we managed to get along.

That summer Moses and I went to work at a family
seafood restaurant, owned by my uncle Bubba, my daddy's
brother, so that we could earn money to purchase school

clothes. It was my last year of middle school. It was my brother Moses's first year at Kashmere High School. Then Mom moved again, from a house across the street from Tom's mother into a two-bedroom apartment three blocks away, off Hirsch Road in Houston.

My resentment against Tom was great, and it would only be a matter of time before there was an incident between the two of us.

One morning it was cold and I wore Tom's sweater to school. Absentmindedly I left it in my locker at school. When I got home, it was late in the day. Mom and Tom were sitting on the couch, and when I walked through the door, Tom stood up, demanding to know if I took something from his room.

I told him I hadn't.

"Where's my sweater?"

"I wore it to school. I'll bring it back tomorrow," I said.

Tom was furious.

"Don't you ever take nothing of mine," he said.

I went off. I lost it. My resentment had gone beyond the boiling point.

"I don't care about your sweater!" I shouted.

I had a bad mouth then, and I cursed him out and charged at him.

"I'll beat you . . . I'll knock you out!" I screamed.

I was in a blind rage.

Tom stepped back, pulled a .22-caliber pistol, and pointed it at me. I wasn't cowed. I picked up a baseball bat, intending to swing it at him.

44

"Hit him!" yelled my brother, who was right behind me. "Get him, Quickie, get him!"

I was lucky Tom didn't shoot me to death. Tom was also lucky I didn't beat him to death with my bat.

My mom ran between us.

"Put that bat down!" she screamed.

She was crying. She took the gun away from Tom.

"Don't you ever pull a gun on my son again," she said. "I just can't do this anymore," she added between loud sobs.

She looked at Tom and then she looked at Moses and me.

"You two guys gotta go."

"*We* have to go?" we said. "You're going to choose *him* over *us*?"

Moses and I were furious. We stormed out, and we hung out with friends on the street all night long. We didn't go to school the next day.

Mom sent Moses and me to live with our paternal grandparents, Betty and George Lofton. Betty had been married to my grandfather Marvin Driver Sr., and after Marvin died, she married George Lofton. Betty and George were willing to take us in. After living in hell on and off the streets with Tom for two years, we broke up as a family. I was in the eighth grade.

The Loftons lived in the Hattiesburg section of Houston in the house where I first met my real dad. Now in my early teens, I had been abandoned by both my parents, and as a substitute for family, I was developing a group of friends in the neighborhood whom I could count on. Among my closest friends were Ray Ray, another kid we called Black, Kory Ross, and a cousin named Michael. We all hung together. I resumed selling drugs and making money stealing cars.

Again I was leading a double life. When you were as poor as I was, and when you saw the fancy cars the drug dealers drove and the spiffy clothes they wore, it stopped being a question of right and wrong. Rather it was a matter of self-esteem and survival. Without my ability to make money on the street I don't know if I could have survived my childhood.

MY GRANDPARENTS, George and Betty, thought I was a good kid. I'm Baptist, and I went to church on Tuesday nights for Bible study. I could name the books of the Bible backward and forward. I went on Wednesday for choir rehearsal, and I went again on Sunday morning for more Bible study and for services the rest of the day.

On Monday I went to school and played football, basketball, or baseball. I was on the drill team, but then after I'd leave school, I'd say to my street friends, "All right, let's go sell some drugs. Let's go steal a car tonight." It was like I was standing on top of a skinny fence wondering, *Which way do I really want to go?*

My grandmother, a strict disciplinarian, had rules for us. I had to be in the house before the streetlights came on or she would lock me out. As I got older, I ignored her rules. Sometimes I'd come back to the house and my key wouldn't open the door because Grandma had double-locked it. I'd knock, but she wouldn't answer it. When that happened, usually I'd jump back in the car with my guys and I'd be gone.

My biological father once tried to intervene in an attempt to get me to walk the straight and narrow. My father, unfortunately, wasn't any sort of role model for me to follow.

"You can't do your grandparents like that," he lectured.

"Whatever," was my lackadaisical, sassy answer.

Had my stepfather Sam still been in my life, perhaps things might have been different. But then again, perhaps not.

I started making good money again selling drugs. I didn't put a dime of it in the bank. I didn't know from banks. I had a lot of money, and I put it underneath my mattress and in a sock drawer. The money was good just to have. I really liked having the money in my pocket. I would walk around with two thousand dollars on me and think I was super-rich. As a teenager it felt like a million dollars.

And I needed the money to buy clothes and more drugs for me to sell.

I REALLY MISSED my mom after she left us with my grandparents. I didn't have a car, and it was too much trouble to borrow one to go to the other side of town, so I'd jump on the city bus right after school just to say hello to her. If she wasn't in her apartment, I'd walk around her neighborhood and ask people, 'Have you seen my mom?'"

"She's over at someone else's house," they'd say, and I'd run over there to find her.

"Hey, baby, are you good?" she'd ask, and I'd get a big hug from her.

If I didn't find my mom I'd get back on the bus to my grandparents' house.

Whenever I saw Tom, I would see red. I couldn't stand him. He was around too much for my taste.

"Mom," I'd say, "you know you don't need him."

"I know," she'd say. "I have to get myself together first."

It was a long time before that happened. As far as I know, my mother's relationship with Tom eventually ended when he went to jail for drugs. For all I know, he may still be locked up.

CHAPTER 3

I'LL PROVE YOU WRONG

I DON'T KNOW why it was so difficult for me to find a male role model when I was growing up. Living in a maternal society seemed to be endemic to the African American community. I was not immune. After my biological father, Marvin, abandoned us, I found out that a total of sixteen other children called him father. He was dad to Tamela, Moses, and me, and over the years I met Marcus, Michael, Sheena, Tina, President, Marvelous, Marcella, and Christopher. There are six others, all very young. I don't know what to tell you, except that it's nuts. I have no animosity. They're still my brothers and sisters.

Sam, who next came into our lives, couldn't keep moving over and over again with my mother, and he eventually dropped away. Tom, as I have said, was a con artist, and because of him Mom turned Moses and me over to my grandparents to raise.

I loved my grandfather George Lofton dearly, but he was so negative and unsupportive that in all the time I lived with him, I don't recall him ever uttering an encouraging word.

Grandpa was a seaman. All his life he traveled on boats, working on container ships and seeing the world. He'd be away for months at a time, sometimes for as long as a year. When he was home he'd say to me, "I don't care about your playing sports. Get an education. I'm going to have to pay for you to go to school. All I care about is that you get that piece of paper," meaning a diploma.

During my entire four-year high school career, he never came to one of my games.

I begged him and begged him. He would always leave me the same phone message: "I don't care about you playing football. All I care about is your getting an education."

I would be so mad at him.

As a high school kid all I heard from him was "You can't."

I spent my entire high school career proving him wrong.

"You know what, Pop," I'd say. "You won't have to pay for anything. I promise you that. I'm going to get a scholarship to go to college."

IT WAS BECAUSE of my grandparents that for the first time in a long time I had some stability in my family life, but I also continued to pursue the street life that allowed me to live better than the average ghetto resident. Because the streets were controlled by gangs from the various neighborhoods, I often carried a gun for my protection. Everyone had them. You didn't go to Dick's Sporting Goods to buy your piece. You didn't go to a pawnshop. You knew someone who had a gun for sale, and you bought it sight unseen without knowing the gun's history, whether it was ever used in a crime. Your gun was your last line of defense in case someone tried to rip you off in a drug deal or rob you on the street.

You also had to protect yourself from drive-by shootings. If a gang from another neighborhood drove into our territory and shot it up, we'd duck and run, and then we'd go and shoot up theirs. I did that a couple of times. I don't think I ever hit anyone, although I never waited around long enough to find out.

Life in the ghetto could be short, in part because there were so many guns around. In high school I lost a friend who was murdered by one of my closest friends. My cousin Black got into an argument over a football jersey with my friend Carlos, and when Black threatened him, Carlos pulled a gun and shot him dead.

Whenever you went to someone else's neighborhood, you took your gun with you. I lived in the Fifth Ward, and my friends and I were wary if we saw someone we didn't know walking our turf. That person might be an undercover cop or someone selling drugs who wasn't supposed to be doing that in our territory.

Likewise, if I was walking down the street in another ward and saw a group of guys standing together on the corner, I'd turn the corner and walk down an alley. If they saw me, they'd want to know, "Where are you from?"

I wouldn't answer. I'd just keep walking, faster and faster.

"Hey, hey, hey," they'd say, and you'd look back and break into a jog. The jog would turn into a sprint, and then it would become a full-out run. Fortunately, I was faster than just about anybody in Houston.

In the part of the city where I was growing up, I would wonder, *Is there anyone I know not selling drugs? Who are the positive role models working a regular job? Who has a degree?*

Until I was about eighteen I couldn't think of anyone

except for my grandparents—my grandfather worked in shipping and my grandmother worked in a hospital—and my mom, who had been a security guard. And my teachers.

Looking back, I realize I easily could have ended up six feet under. My brother Moses and I turned out to be among the lucky ones.

AFTER I MOVED in with my grandparents, I went to Milby High School, an inner-city school in southeast Houston. The middle schools I attended had mostly African American students. Milby was 95 percent Hispanic, the rest African American. African Americans and Hispanics were wary of one another.

I got into a lot of fights at Milby. When I arrived there as a freshman, I asked myself, *Do I really want to be here?*

It was one of the crossroads of my life. I could have gone either way. It would have been very easy for me to drop out of school and turn to selling drugs full-time. But I had two things going for me. I was a good student, and I was an exceptional athlete. I could run like the wind, and I could jump higher than just about anyone in the school.

I played sports because of my older brother Moses, who was one of the most kindhearted, compassionate guys I've ever known, especially when it comes to family. When I was a kid, Moses, who was a year older than me, was my hero. He was the guy I always wanted to be like. Since I didn't have that father figure, he was the one I always followed. If he went somewhere, I wanted to be with him. If he played a sport, I wanted to play the same sport with him.

Moses was the first one to play football. I wanted to play because he played it, and of course my dad had played it. And when Moses started to play basketball, I wanted to play it, too, because I wanted to follow in his footsteps.

My brother Marvin was one of the best high school basketball players I ever saw. He probably would have gone to the pros, but then at Milby High he broke his leg. After that he lived his dreams through me, and I lived my dreams through him, because of the relationship we had. We have a bond that will never be broken. Right now he's a lieutenant on the staff of a state penitentiary in Texas.

Sports gave me purpose and allowed me to graduate with a degree and go on to bigger things. When I was a little kid Moses and I ran for the Wings AAU track team. In high school I high-jumped, long-jumped, triple-jumped, and ran on the relay team. I was pretty fast but I didn't become world class until I got to college.

In baseball I was an outfielder and swung the bat pretty good. I'd get on base, and then steal another. In basketball I was the varsity center because even though I was only five foot ten, I could jump higher than anyone else on the team. The Milby basketball team made the playoffs the four years I was there. My teammates played college ball at some of the smaller Division IAA and Division II schools. I did set one Texas high school record: I was responsible for fifty-three charges in one season. An opposing player would run into me as I guarded the basket, I'd hit the deck, and a charging foul would be called on him. I doubt that record will ever be broken.

It was in football that I really shone. My freshman year I was a running back on the junior varsity, but when the varsity team made the playoffs head coach Mike Truelove brought me up as a wide receiver. It was a smart move on his part. I only weighed a hundred pounds, but I was so fast no one could catch me. In a game against Austin, I was open and would have scored a touchdown, but I had no experience and dropped the pass. I should have caught it, but I never even touched the ball. It was a lesson: I needed to learn how to catch the football.

My biological father helped me do that. One of the side benefits of playing football was that it gave me the chance to reconnect with my dad. I was living in his parents' home, and so my dad would come and visit periodically, and he and I'd go out back and play catch. Dad had had a bunch of kids with different mothers, and he was trying to be a father to them, so I appreciated his taking the time to spend time with me.

I derived a great deal of joy from having dad throw the football to me in the backyard. He still had a great arm, and it gave me the opportunity to practice catching bulletlike passes from a quarterback who could really wing it.

My dad and I never had as loving a relationship as I would have liked, but we always had a bond through football, and it continued all the way through my college career.

· · ·

EVEN AS AN adult, I am conflicted about my relationship with my father.

We've had rocky times, but I will always support him. In 2008, he was harassed by police officers in Houston. No one knows exactly what happened.

My father said he was at my grandmother's house. He was getting ready to leave—but he saw the police. So he decided not to leave and pulled the car back into my grandmother's driveway and planned to wait until they left. The police came anyway. They asked him for his identification and all that. Why? No one knows. Keep in mind, most of the Houston police know who my dad is and know my family pretty well. My family sold drugs throughout my childhood; we were all dealing drugs or stealing cars. My dad, uncles, aunts, cousins. No one in my family besides my grandparents worked a normal job; everyone else was in the streets.

So the police came after my father. I don't know if they asked him if he had anything or what. They said he was resisting arrest; he said he wasn't. He said they hit the top of his head when they threw him in the back of the squad car. He said he barely remembered anything after that, just that he was floating in and out of consciousness. He remembers the cops took him to a store, and, according to my dad, made him take some crack cocaine. They were trying to stuff it into his mouth—that was the story he gave me.

My dad is a diabetic, and everyone said by the time he got to the police station, he was unconscious. He had completely blacked out in the backseat. That's why he was rushed to the hospital. Doctors got him breathing and put him on oxygen.

Of course, while he was in the hospital they said my father had crack cocaine in his system, and that he had put it there.

The thing is, my dad had never taken drugs before—so why would he put crack cocaine in his system? Everybody had their side of the story.

The police internal affairs investigators didn't know exactly what happened, and my dad's attorneys tried to challenge it. I told my dad I would help him to find out the truth. The thing that got me about the whole thing was that the police were coming after me—through my father.

I jumped on a private plane with Tina to fly down there. The media was waiting at the airport but I continued on to my dad. The doctors took the breathing tube out of his mouth so he could breathe on his own again. He told me that one of the cops said, "Yeah, I didn't like your son anyway." My dad said this cop, whoever he was, had gone to school with me and he didn't like me. He was telling my dad that—as he was beating him up. My dad said that was one of the last things he remembered before they bashed his head against the car and he passed out.

A day later I went back and looked after my dad. He was still in the hospital but was improving. However, his story changed. It became "The hospital had me all drugged up from different things." That was when I thought, *Okay, maybe Dad doesn't remember things exactly the way they happened.*

The thing is, my dad didn't want me to spend money to find out what the truth was, so he decided to just drop the case against the police. And that's about where we left it. He was never found guilty. The way it stands now, I still have my questions. I'm going to believe my father. Of course I will. He could be telling the truth. To this day, he says he remembers the cops giving him crack cocaine and the police mentioning my name when they were beating him up—because the cops didn't like me.

It's not the only time that my past life, and what I did in my youth, have come up. Sometimes it makes life very, very complicated.

MY MILBY HIGH SCHOOL football team made the playoffs my freshman and sophomore years, but we were never a powerhouse the way we were in basketball. My junior year we didn't win a single football game, and we finished 6-4 when I was senior.

We had a handful of great players, but as a team we weren't very good. Our quarterback was Andre Credit, whom I was close to all through high school. Andre and I made for a devastating combination. He would throw it up, and I would leap or dive or run to catch it.

We scored a lot of touchdowns, especially in our last year together, when I was a junior and he was a senior, but it still wasn't good enough for us to win games. I was one of the top pass catchers in Texas football my senior year—in one game I caught three touchdowns—but we weren't the sort of team that college coaches would come and scout. No one came to look at me that I can remember.

My grandmother has a scrapbook full of clippings of me making diving catches and scoring touchdowns, but I have never looked at it. I had caught twenty touchdown passes my senior year, but it didn't occur to me that I was a great athlete—that didn't happen until I made it in the NFL. All I cared about was making my grandfather happy, using sports—football, basketball, or track—to gain a scholarship to college. My goal was to be the first child on my father's side to go to college, but my intention was to get there because of my education and not because of sports. Oh, like most kids I could dream. As far back as middle school, when I ran track for the Wings track team, I thought about becoming a track star and taking my family out of poverty. When I got older, I heard about the possibility of getting drafted by the pros, but I didn't know how possible that really was. I wasn't that big into football when I was in high school. I played it, but I didn't study it. A lot of kids today watch sports, sports, sports all the time on TV or their iPad. When I was a kid I wasn't a big TV watcher. I was always in the streets.

Different guys in high school would ask me, "What are you planning on doing?"

"What are you talking about?" I'd ask them.

For me sports was a means to gain an education. I figured I'd graduate from college and work for one of the big accounting firms when I graduated.

Maybe one day I'll own a big accounting firm, I posited.

That was where I was heading. In high school I never thought seriously about playing in the NBA or in the NFL. But I could dream. Yes, I would say to myself, *Maybe I will and maybe I won't. If the opportunity comes, I'll make the best of it.* But in high school I was using sports to get that scholarship to go to college so I could say to my grandfather, "Yeah,

I told you so. You're not going to have to pay to send me to college. And I *will* have a degree."

It was only after I got to college that I got serious about my education. I played football in college, and I dreamed of making it in the pros, but I also knew that dreams don't always come true. I knew that if I got a great education no one could ever take that away from me.

UP UNTIL THE fall of my senior year of high school I suffered deep disappointment because it appeared that no college was interested in recruiting me except Alcorn State, an all-black college located somewhere in Mississippi. Andre Credit, my quarterback at Milby High, had gone to Alcorn, and he had told the coaching staff to come down and look at me, which they did. The head coach and offensive coordinator drove to Houston to meet with me and my grandparents.

The coach, Carnell Jones, gave me a booklet about the Alcorn State football team. Quarterback Steve McNair was on the cover.

"You know," Jones said, "McNair is up for the Heisman. We're a passing school. If you come to us, we're going to get you the ball a lot."

He also offered me a full scholarship.

One day not long afterward I came home from school and noticed my grandmother going through the mail. For our extended family Grandma was the central post office. Uncle Bubba, whose real name was Marion, had his mail sent to her address. Uncle Winston had his mail sent to her address. Aunts and uncles, too. A lot of the family's mail went to her.

"Quickie," she said to me, "I keep getting all these letters for Donald Driver. I don't know this person. Who is Donald Driver?"

I was taken aback.

"What did you say, Grandma?"

She held up a stack of envelopes two inches thick.

"See," she said. "Donald Driver, Donald Driver, Donald Driver."

"Granny," I said, "I'm Donald Driver."

"Your name is Quickie Jerome Driver," she said.

My whole life she had never called me anything but Quickie. No one else called me Donald, either. I was known by everyone as Quickie.

"Granny," I said, "my given name is Donald Jerome Driver."

In a box was a stack of letters from college coaches inquiring whether I would be interested in accepting scholarships. There were letters from some big schools—the University of Miami, Texas A&M, and the University of Michigan—plus actual scholarship offers from schools like the University of Arkansas, Arkansas State, Western Missouri, Blinn Junior College, and other small schools and junior colleges.

I had had my heart set on going to the University of Miami, but Miami hadn't offered me a scholarship.

February 2 was the signing date. It was also my birthday. Miami didn't call, but Alcorn State did, and I agreed to accept their scholarship offer.

Not long afterward I got calls from Miami and Texas A&M offering me full scholarships.

I wanted to go to Miami very badly, but I had already told Alcorn I was going to go there. I was still considering Miami when my grandfather said to me one day, "Son, I want you to go to a black college. I'm not sure how you're going to be treated if you go to an all-white school. Make my dream come true. Please go to a black college."

Grandpa had been kind enough to let us come live with him, and I didn't want to let him down. I spurned Miami and accepted the scholarship to Alcorn State. In the fall of 1994 my grandmother and my uncle Winston drove me to Lorman, Mississippi, the home of Alcorn State University, a country school in the middle of absolutely nowhere. How country was it? There was not a single McDonald's or Burger King or any other fast-food restaurant in the entire town. If you wanted groceries, you had to drive fifteen minutes to Port Gibson.

Because of her work schedule, my grandmother dropped me off at my dorm two days before the rest of the freshman football players arrived. Fortunately, Andre Credit, my old QB at Milby, was there, or else I'd have been the loneliest kid on campus. Andre had grown up with me at Milby, and Goree White, who played football with me in high school and was also on the Alcorn team, grew up with me in the Fifth Ward. Goree and I would room together throughout my college career.

When practice began, I was privileged to play on the same team with Steve McNair, who at the end of the year was drafted in the first round by the Houston Oilers. During practice, Steve threw me a pass that I caught, and as the defender was coming up to tackle me, I pointed as though I were instructing one of my offensive linemen to block him, and when the defender went for the ruse, looking to see who was coming, I made a spin move, got around him, and scored. I was amazed the move worked. It also gave me an idea I could play on the college level.

The fall of my freshman year was also when I went bald. It wasn't my choice—at first. It was the week of freshman hazing for the football players. One of my freshman roommates was a linebacker and he had been growing his dreds since he was a baby. The upperclassmen didn't care. They shaved it all off. When they came for me on receivers' night, I was helpless to do anything. They grabbed me, held me down, and cut off all my hair.

I would walk around campus, and the students would see my bald head and say, "You're obviously a freshman." But I got a positive response from the girls on campus. They liked it.

"You look cute with your bald head," a number of girls said to me.

I'm not stupid. I've been bald ever since.

FRESHMAN YEAR I also fell in love. We used to have fraternity dance contests called step shows, and I was walking back to my dorm from one of these step shows when I ran into a very beautiful coed named Alandra, who looked like Betty Boop. When you fall for someone so attractive, you sometimes think she's the right person. We started dating, and she could be a terrific person, but there was something wrong with her. She could be happy one moment, and five minutes later she'd just turn mean.

Being what I considered to be a good man, I was thinking I could fix it.

I really care about her, I thought to myself. *I can make her change.*

She would talk to me about the abusive relationships she had had, and I suppose because I was a football player, she figured I'd be abusive, too. But I wasn't one of those men who hit women. I suspect it was what she wanted me to do, but I never would give in to her.

She would pick fights, but I would never engage her. If she tried to hit me I'd hold her down until she calmed down.

The summer after my freshman year she came home with me to Houston. We lived at my mom's house.

One day Alandra became angry.

"I'm tired of this," she said. "I'm leaving."

"Okay," I said. "You can leave if that's what you want."

"Why aren't you mad?" she wanted to know.

"I'm not mad," I said. "If you want to go back to Mississippi, go back to Mississippi."

She swung at me, and I held her down on the bed until she calmed down. My mom ran in to see what the commotion was all about.

"My son is not going to hit you," she said. "If you can't deal with that, then you need to get out of this."

Alandra left and went to stay with one of my mom's friends for a week. We worked it out and got back together.

"I'm not the type of guy you've been with," I told her. "I'm not going to hit you. I'm not going to degrade you. That's not me.

"You found a good man," I continued. "If you don't want that, you have to make a choice."

It wouldn't be too long before Alandra made that choice.

I CONTINUED TO deal drugs at college, and here's why. The summer after my freshman year, I'd briefly worked at the Family Dollar store, earning minimum wage, and then I went to work in a factory on an assembly line. I made pipes, putting on a coil, screwing it in, and painting it. I worked from seven in the morning until three in the afternoon at this mindless task, and for my efforts I was paid a grand total of eight dollars an hour. At the end of the week I was lucky if my paycheck amounted to two hundred dollars after they took out taxes. By the end of the summer I had made up my mind that I no longer could do a job like that. I realized that working a normal nine-to-five job was not something I wanted to do. When a friend of mine asked me if I wanted to work at the Burger King down the street from my grandmother, I thanked him but firmly told him no.

After freshman year I returned to the streets, continuing to sell drugs and to steal cars until it was time for me to return to college for my sophomore year. I was no longer selling for J.R. I was working for myself.

I realized that the drug of choice at Alcorn State was marijuana, so I switched to selling that, and I was glad I did. If I had gotten caught selling harder drugs, I would have faced real time. The penalty for marijuana wasn't nearly as harsh, though it wasn't exactly light, either.

I felt differently about dealing drugs in college than I did in high school once I became a varsity athlete. When I was in high school I knew that if I got caught with drugs, I was only going to a juvenile facility. Maybe I'd have done a year or two. When I got to college and became a star athlete, I realized I could seriously jeopardize my career if I get caught with marijuana or alcohol or was arrested for drunken driving. As a result I was more afraid in college than I was when I was in high school or middle school. I went to great pains to make sure I knew whom I was selling to.

I WENT INTO a partnership with Goree White, my friend and roommate, and another friend, Benny. We'd buy a large supply of marijuana, and after we sold it, we'd split the money three ways.

No one in my family knew I had money. My dad gave me five hundred toward the purchase of a beat-up Oldsmobile. I put up the other five hundred, and then I spent a grand on tires and rims. I put an expensive sound system inside it. I bought nice clothes, and I threw parties for my teammates and friends. As fast as the money came in, that's how fast it went out. Drug dealers don't put their money in the bank, buy stocks, or open an individual retirement account.

I only tried using marijuana once in college. I smoked a joint and afterward all I wanted to do was eat! And sleep.

Is this what it does? I wondered. I couldn't figure out what the big deal was.

I never smoked it again.

But I sold it. Pounds and pounds of it.

I was never arrested—never even close—in college, but I did get robbed a couple of times. One time I went into a club and someone broke into my car and stole all of my stuff, including my stash of marijuana.

Another time two guys came to my dorm room and knocked on my door. I had just gotten back from Houston, and I was bagging up the marijuana. I opened the door.

"What's up?" I asked.

"Hey, man, you got something for us?" one of them asked.

"No," I said. "I don't know what you're talking about."

"Your name is Quickie, right?"

"Yeah."

"I don't have anything," I said. "I don't know what you're talking about."

I didn't know them, and I wasn't about to be caught in a sting. I closed the door and they left.

Twenty minutes later they knocked again and I opened the door.

"Goree told us this is where we can come," one of them said.

Goree was my roommate, and I figured Goree had sent them, so stupidly I let one of them in. I told the other guy to stay outside. I turned my back to my prospective buyer when

I went to lock the door, and when I turned around the guy had pulled a gun on me.

"Where's the money?" he barked. "Where's the marijuana?"

I pointed to the table.

"It's right there, dummy," I said.

"Bag it up," he said.

I just looked at him. If he wanted it, he was going to have to bag it himself.

My gun was in my bag, but I wasn't about to reach for it. I thought, *You're either going to shoot me, or you're going to run out of here before I shoot you.*

"You gotta have *something*," he said.

I had four hundred dollars' worth of marijuana already bagged up. He grabbed that and two large piles of loose marijuana that I hadn't yet bagged.

He pointed the gun at me, unlocked the door while facing me, and walked out the door. He and his buddy took off down the hallway.

I ran and got my gun with the intention of going after them, but I realized it wasn't worth having a shoot-out inside the dorm. I chased them, but all I could do was watch as they jumped into their car and took off.

AT ALCORN STATE I participated in football, the sport I loved, and track, the sport in which I was gifted. The track coach discovered me in the gym shooting hoops early in my sophomore year. He walked by as I dunked the ball. I was wearing flip-flops when I did it.

He figured with my leaping ability I'd be a natural in the broad jump, the high jump, and the triple jump. I also performed in the decathlon, a grueling two days of running, jumping, and throwing things like the shotput and the javelin. I was very good at all those disciplines. At Alcorn State I was the Southwestern Athletic Conference indoor and outdoor champion in the long jump, triple jump, and decathlon. I was named the outstanding field performer for the indoor and outdoor season in 1996, 1997, and 1998. No one could beat me.

My sophomore year I finished first at the Pelican Relays, held at Southern University in Baton Rouge, in the high jump with a jump of seven feet, six and a half inches, earning me the number-one ranking in the NCAAs and qualifying me for the U.S. Olympic track and field trials, which were held in Atlanta in the summer of 1995.

We should have flown from Alcorn State to Atlanta, but our coach decided to go on the cheap, and we drove the whole way, 460 miles along Interstate 20, past Jackson, Mississippi, and Birmingham, Alabama. The good thing was I was allowed to bring my dad, my fiancée, Alandra, and my little brother Christopher along with me. Someplace in Alabama we stopped at a Pizza Hut to eat.

I was in the parking lot when I turned around to see where Christopher was, and when I turned back I walked smack on face first into the ends of a stack of wooden two-by-fours that were sticking out from a parked pickup truck. I grabbed my eye, and when I took my hand off, I was bleeding badly. Blood ran down my face in rivulets, down the front of my shirt, and onto the ground. My eye began swelling, and my vision became blurry. I was in such terrible pain that I couldn't eat, couldn't do anything. I feared I wouldn't be able to perform at the Olympic trials.

My father pleaded with Coach Alecia Shields to take me to the hospital and get stitched up, but she insisted we drive on to Atlanta. I lay down in the backseat with my head in Alandra's lap. With the help of some New-Skin that we bought at a gas station the bleeding finally stopped.

At the trials I passed my physical exam. I had a patch over my eye, but I could jump with it. I looked like a pirate.

The trials were a disaster. I had three tries at seven foot two, a height I consistently jumped. I missed on all three. Nevertheless, there was a silver lining. I didn't get to go to the Olympics, but because I had made the trip I also avoided going to jail.

Back on campus the cops had raided my room. When I returned from Atlanta, I found my room completely cleaned out. The TV was gone. Everything.

I've been robbed, was my first thought.

But it wasn't a robbery. Someone had evidently tipped the police off that we were selling drugs from our dorm room, and they had come into our room with a warrant and took everything as evidence. They busted my roomie Goree White and Benny, a mutual friend, for possession of ten pounds of marijuana. Goree was more talented than I was in football. We were both wide receivers on the football team, and we were taking summer classes. Goree, Benny, and I were also selling marijuana together.

I wasn't arrested because I wasn't there.

Benny took the rap for Goree. That's part of the code of the hood. You never let good friends down. He took the rap for Goree because he felt Goree had a future in football. Benny told the cops, "My friends had nothing to do with this. It was my stash."

Goree never did make it in pro football. Instead he found trouble. The first time he went to jail, I paid his lawyer's fees to get him out. The last time he got out, I made sure he had decent clothes and shoes. He has beautiful kids. I hope he knows now there's a better life for him and that he tries to strive for it.

CHAPTER 4

TINA
AND THE
NFL
DRAFT

WHILE A STUDENT at Alcorn State I met Tina, the love of my life. We had met several times before we began dating. She was a freshman who had won a scholarship for her skill playing the clarinet. She was also trying out for the dance team. During two-a-days football practice the band would be practicing nearby in an area we called the Yard, and one day I noticed this beautiful girl with short hair in white tights marching with the band.

I knew some of the other members of the dance team, and I asked one of them to hook me up with her. She wouldn't, saying the girl already had a boyfriend who went to Jackson State.

"Tina loves her boyfriend," she said. "She doesn't want to deal with you."

I wasn't giving up.

Not long afterward I saw her walking from class up a hill to her dorm.

"Tina!" I hollered at her. "Come here, girl!"

Smooth I wasn't.

She turned around, looked at me, and kept walking.

I had friends walking with me, and I was embarrassed.

"Nobody wants you anyway!" I yelled at her.

After that I didn't see her for a long time.

I had been engaged to Alandra for a year and a half at

the time, and it was right about this time that she left me for her high school sweetheart. I was heartbroken because I did love her. But God put it in my heart that she wasn't the right person, and from there we moved on. She is married now to her high school sweetheart. I have to think she has said to herself, at least once, *I messed up. I had a good guy.*

A year went by, and I was playing the field. I wasn't looking to be attached to anyone. Then I saw Tina again. By now I was a known quantity, a player on the football team. I had enough status for her to stop and talk to me.

She had a tomboy haircut.

"Why did you cut your hair?" I asked her.

"You like it?" she asked.

"It looks real cute like that," I said. "You look like Halle Berry."

"Do I?"

She asked if I would help the dance team train at the gym.

I don't want to train them, I thought, *but I certainly will work out with you.*

She and I and a couple of other members of the dance team met at the training center every day at a set time. Tina was never late. I was friends with one of the other girls on the dance team, and I didn't realize it, but Tina was jealous. She started not showing up for training.

I had to call her, and when she asked me about my interest in the other girl, I told her I only had eyes for her, Tina.

I asked her what she was looking for in a man.

"I want somebody who's going to love me for me," she said. "I want someone affectionate and passionate."

I couldn't help but note the difference between Tina and Alandra. All Tina wanted was someone to love her, a man who loved only her, a man who just wanted to be with her.

"You're looking at your man," I said. "I'm your guy."

She still had that boyfriend, who had graduated and was living in Monroe, Louisiana, and I convinced her to choose me instead.

"I don't know what the future holds for me," I told her, "but I promise to give you everything you ask for."

I met her dad, mom, and brother, and we all fell in love. I realized this was going to be something special.

I was still selling drugs, but I didn't want her to know that, so I figured this was no time to show off that I had money. On our first date we went to McDonald's. After we ate, we went to the movies to see *The Nutty Professor,* starring Eddie Murphy. She fell asleep in the middle.

Things were going so well between us, and I knew it would be only a matter of time before she found out about my drug dealing. All my life I had played both sides of the fence. I was a good person, and I was a drug dealer. I was a Christian, and I was a car thief. I was one and the other. Until Tina came into my life.

One day I asked Tina to hide a large duffel bag for me in her room.

She was hesitant.

"Don't open it," I said. "Just put it in your dorm room. I'll get it later."

"What is it?" she wanted to know.

"Just . . . put . . . it . . . in . . . your . . . room," I pleaded.

She knew exactly what it was.

Tina wasn't like the girls from my neighborhood who would have said, "Oh, I've got ya, baby. You're good. Go do what you have to do."

If Tina had been that girl, I'd still be the same guy playing on both sides of the fence. If Tina had been that girl, who knows if I would have made it to the NFL.

Tina came from a Christian middle-class family. She had a mom and dad who were very supportive, who taught her that school and education came first and that hanging out with the bad boys could only lead to misery. She gave me an ultimatum.

"If you want to be with me," Tina said, "you've got to stop this."

Meaning I had to get out of the drug business.

"God is testing you," she said. "You have to make a choice."

The choice was not an easy one. After Tina told me she wasn't going to hold my stash of drugs for me, my first reaction was not to be with Tina anymore. That was my mindset.

I talked to my boys in Houston and on campus, and they were telling me, "There are more fish in the sea. Tina isn't the only fish out there. Don't worry about her. Just keep doing what you're doing. Don't let this girl change who you are."

I don't need her, I told myself. *I can do this by myself.*

But as time went on, I realized how much I loved her. The more I was with her, the more I realized how honest she was and how passionate. Tina didn't care how much money I had. It wasn't about what I could buy her, because I wasn't buying her anything. It wasn't about what I had or what I was doing. All she cared about was loving me. And that's when I realized she was the one. *The drug thing is over,* I told myself. *I'm out of the game.*

This was a crossroads. But quitting the drug business isn't the same as quitting your job at McDonald's. When I went back to the Fifth Ward and told my suppliers I was getting out of the game, they tried hard to talk me out of it.

"Noooo," they said, "you can't get out. Once you're in, you're in."

For three days they kept me hostage trying to get me to change my mind. They didn't pull guns, but they broke out every trick and mind game they could think of to talk me out of quitting. When they saw I was holding my ground, their final words to me were "If you're not part of the game, we don't know if you can hang out with us anymore."

It was a sad moment. I was leaving behind the life that I had known since I was a boy living next door to J.R.

"I'm always going to be part of the hood," I told them, "but I'm going to have to separate the hood from where I want to be."

In a way I was heartbroken. But I knew it was a small price to pay. And now when I see these fellows, they say, "Hey, Quickie, come around with us," and I say, "Oh no, you be good. See you later." I don't want the police to think I'm involved with them. As long as I'm just hanging out, I'm just Donald Driver back in my neighborhood.

When I finally screwed up the courage to tell Goree White I was getting out of the drug game, he felt betrayed.

"Man," he said, "you can't let a chick change who you are."

But I felt with Tina I would have a better life for myself.

Later, after I had made it in the NFL and was making decent money, an uncle of mine who was a big drug dealer in Houston called and asked me if I would be interested in going back into the business.

"You know," he said, "this is a great opportunity for you to make some good money. With the money you have, you can go back into the drug game. You now have the finances to buy a lot of drugs."

I thought about it. I was sorely tempted. It was also an opportunity to help my uncle, who once had a Corvette, a Mercedes, and a fine house. He had never put money away for tough times, and he needed the money to get back on his feet. I loved my uncle to death, and I wanted to help him.

I talked to Tina.

"I think I'm going to take my first paycheck and give it to my uncle," I told her. "He's going to pay me back, but I'm also going to make a significant amount of money."

"No," Tina said. "God don't like ugly."

She pleaded with me not to jeopardize my football career by making a loan to a drug dealer.

"Donald, no. It isn't worth it," she said. "We're not doing that. God has blessed you to be in this position. If you help out your uncle, and it's discovered, it could be alleged that Donald Driver was the supplier. Even if you have nothing to do with the transaction, even if you aren't doing anything illegal, someone could always say you financed the deal."

I went back to my uncle, and buttressed by Tina's strong

will, I told him I couldn't do it. Oh, it's hard to turn down your family. But I believed it was a test, and I'm not sure I'd be where I am today if I had done that.

TINA AND I started dating in July, and I proposed to her in September. You know how you know when it's just the right person for you? I knew Tina was the one for me.

I proposed to Tina twice. The first time was in my brother's closet. Don't ask me why. I was nervous. I had stopped dealing drugs. Like most drug dealers, I had spent all the money I made on my lifestyle, booze, parties, expensive things I didn't need, and by the time I proposed to her I was broke like every other normal college student.

"Tina, will you marry me?" I asked, and I handed her a ring that looked like it might have come from a Cracker Jack box. It had a chip of a diamond, never mind a diamond.

"Yes," she said, "I will marry you, but what is this?"

She looked at the ring.

"Okay, thank you," she said, but I knew she didn't really think much of it.

I had received a Pell Grant worth $1,650, and I decided to put my Pell Grant money to a very good use. I drove to Vicksburg, Mississippi, to search the pawnshops for a suitable diamond engagement ring.

They had a nice, big one-carat diamond set in gold that I could have for $1,200.

I returned to campus, and later Tina and I headed by car

81

for Houston. We stopped at a McDonald's in Lafayette, Louisiana, where I got on my knees and proposed for the second time. This time I had a ring more worthy of her. She loved it.

We were married two years later.

IN MY FOUR years of playing football at Alcorn State, we had our best team my freshman year, when Steve McNair led us to an 8-2-1 regular season record. In his last regular season game against Jackson State, Steve completed 29 of 34 passes for 533 yards and five touchdowns. Unfortunately, we went up against Youngstown State in the playoffs, and we were clobbered 63–20. Even though Steve threw for the three scores, our shellacking cost him the Heisman Trophy. He finished third in the voting behind Colorado running back Rashaan Salaan.

After McNair left, the Alcorn State team had mediocre records the rest of the way. We won only four games each of my last three seasons. Even so, we were an exciting ballclub on offense. We played against the bump-and-run, as most of the all-black colleges did. We spread the receivers, and when the ball was hiked, we ran like the wind. The cornerbacks would bump you hard, trying to knock you off course. They played man-to-man all day. With my speed and jumping ability, I was able to catch 88 passes for 1,932 yards and 17 touchdowns.

A few of those touchdowns were particularly memorable. We played Southern University at Southern on a rainy day when the rain was just pouring down. As the half was coming to an end, our QB, Mose Lemon, threw a Hail Mary from around the fifty-yard line. I jumped up and made the catch in the end zone, and as I celebrated I wondered why our fans were so quiet. The penalty flag lay on the ground. One of our linemen had been caught for holding. There was a ten-yard penalty, and the play was called back.

We went back into the huddle, and Mose called for the exact same play. He threw it up again, and again I made a leaping grab, getting in front of the defender and wrestling it away for a touchdown. As I ran into the locker room I was floating on air.

Toward the end of the season in my senior year we played Mississippi Valley State, Jerry Rice's alma mater. At the end of that game I made a diving catch in the back of the end zone and scored the touchdown that won the game 23–18.

In the final game of my college career we played powerhouse Jackson State. Playing for Jackson State were two touted juniors, wide receiver Sylvester Morris and defensive back Rashard Anderson. Morris would be taken by the Kansas City Chiefs and Anderson by the Carolina Panthers in the first round of the NFL draft. I had a better game than both of them, and I was hoping that my senior-year play would be good enough to attract attention from the pros.

The highlight of the Jackson State game came after it was over. There to greet me was my grandfather, George Lofton, who hadn't attended a single game of mine in either high school or college because of his stubborn insistence that my education was more important than my playing sports. Yes, I resented him all through my high school and college years, but when I became older, I came to understand him. Today when I visit schools, I tell the kids, "Get your education. No one can take that from you. Sports can be taken away in a split second."

I always took what my grandfather had said very seriously. I got good grades, kept up a 3.0 average, and earned an accounting degree at Alcorn State. I was in the middle of pursuing a degree in computer science when the 1999 draft rolled around.

MY SENIOR YEAR I began looking at my competition to see which college players were entering the NFL player draft, especially the top receivers in the draft. I remember watching David Boston of Ohio State, and I also watched Torry Holt of North Carolina State. Another receiver, Troy Edwards of Louisiana Tech, had 405 yards receiving in a game against Nebraska. I figured my 1,932 yards and 17 touchdowns were comparable to theirs, and so I figured I should have been at least among the top eight receivers to go pro.

We held scout day at Alcorn State in front of a group of pro scouts, and I ran a 4.49, 4.5 and 4.48 forty. I ran great routes and caught the ball well. Fourteen NFL scouts were there, and all of them talked to me. Two days later the Green Bay Packers actually sent Alonzo Highsmith, who had once starred as a running back, to work me out.

The San Francisco 49ers called me to say they were going to pick me. The receivers coach called and spoke to my dad.

"We're thinking about Donald," the coach said.

"The Forty-Niners have a fourth-round pick," my dad told me, "and that's where they're going to pick you."

The Kansas City Chiefs flew me in for a tryout, and they told me they were considering taking me in the fourth or fifth round. I was cool with that.

I said to Tina, my fiancée at the time, "Most likely I'll be drafted on the second day."

I, MY DAD, Tina, my future father-in-law, and ten other family members sat around my dad's house in front of the TV the first day of the draft waiting for the phone to ring.

"Don't go anywhere," Dad said to me. "Wait here."

I watched on ESPN as a group of wide receivers were taken in the first round. The St. Louis Rams took Torry Holt, the Arizona Cardinals picked David Boston, the Pittsburgh Steelers took Troy Edwards, and in the second round the Cleveland Browns took Kevin Johnson of Syracuse and the Buffalo Bills took Peerless Price of Tennessee.

I was disappointed but not crushed, because both San Francisco and Kansas City said I would probably go the second day of the draft.

I was back at my dad's house the next day when I watched more wide receivers get drafted. The Chicago Bears took two wide receivers, D'Wayne Bates of Northwestern and Marty Booker of Louisiana-Monroe.

Louisiana-Monroe? I thought.

Then the Seattle Seahawks took Karsten Bailey of Auburn. He was the eighth wide receiver taken before me. What was going on?

Denver took Travis McGriff of Florida, and then in the

fourth round Craig Yeast of Kentucky went to Cincinnati, Dameane Douglas of California went to Oakland, and Brandon Stokley of Louisiana-Lafayette went to Baltimore.

Louisiana-Lafayette?

I was beginning to panic.

When the Kansas City Chiefs, the team that had invited me for a tryout and said I'd probably be taken in the fourth or fifth round, took Larry Parker of USC instead, I couldn't take it any longer.

"Bye, Pop," I said, and I fled his house and drove over to my grandparents' home to wait out the rest of the afternoon.

Two other wide receivers, Wane McGarity of Texas and Na Brown of North Carolina, were then picked by Dallas and Philadelphia, respectively.

At the day's end I was undrafted and devastated.

My mind was awhirl.

I was thinking, *I played football all these years to better my life. All this time I was thinking this would be my opportunity. Teams were telling me something was going to happen, but nothing does.*

This is it, I told myself. *Thank God I have an accounting degree. I might as well get ready to start sending my applications to accounting firms.*

Round five went by, and three more wide receivers were taken, and then round six, when three more went, including MarTay Jenkins of Nebraska-Omaha.

I was feeling very low.

I let my family down, I was thinking. *I didn't do what I was supposed to do.*

I tried to think of why I had fallen so low. Maybe it was because I was twenty-four years old. Maybe it was because Alcorn State had had such a mediocre record and the scouts didn't think I had played against top competition. Maybe . . .

Outside my grandparents' house I was playing football in the street with my brothers and cousins. My dad had asked them to be with me, to calm me down. I was feeling really miserable, certain I had failed everyone.

"Hey, Quickie, the Green Bay Packers are on the phone!" yelled my dad.

"Yeah, right, whatever," I said, thinking he was pulling my leg.

"Boy, I'm serious," he said.

It was Ron Wolf, the Packers' general manager.

"We have the 212 and 213 pick," he said. "We're going to take you at 213."

"Take me at 212," I pleaded. I was feeling so underappreciated I was fishing for any sort of leg up.

"No," he said. "We're going to take a guy you played against at 212, Chris Akins from Arkansas–Pine Bluff."

"Why don't you take me at 212 and him at 213?" I said. "I'm *way* better than he is. Go back and watch the game we played against each other. I *killed* him in the game."

"He's not a better player than me," said another voice.

I didn't realize it, but Chris Akins was on the line, too.

"Don't worry about it, Donald," Ron Wolf said. "It's not going to change anything."

I was fussing because I felt I should have been an early-round pick.

"Your name is going to come across the TV screen any moment," Wolf said.

After it did, I said, "Thank you," and I hung up the phone. The Packers called right back.

"You have to talk to the media," I was told.

On the phone I told the reporters, "I'll get an opportunity to play in the National Football League, something I've always dreamed about doing. I intend to come in and work hard in the hopes that I can make the team."

I said all the right things, but I was mad at the world. I felt I should have been drafted much higher. Not only that, but I was mad when I found out I was going to Green Bay, a town where I was going to freeze my butt off. I knew they had won a Super Bowl, that Brett Favre was there, but I had never been much of a Packers fan. Being from Texas I had rooted for the Houston Oilers and the Dallas Cowboys.

Where the hell am I going? I wondered.

But in the end, I was indeed looking forward to playing in the NFL.

"We just might get the dream I was always looking for," I told my family.

CHAPTER 5

MAKING
IT

WHEN I WAS drafted I didn't even know where Green Bay was. I knew it was north. I knew it was cold. I was thinking it was in Illinois, somewhere north of Chicago.

It didn't take me long, however, to learn that Green Bay was in fact in the state of Wisconsin and that the Packers had won more league championships than any other NFL team, with thirteen at the time I joined the team in the summer of 1999. The Packers had won Super Bowls in 1967 and 1968 under Vince Lombardi, one of the most famous and successful coaches in the history of the game, and had won a Super Bowl in 1997 under coach Mike Holmgren.

The Packers were founded in 1919 by George Calhoun, whom most people have never heard of, and coach Earl "Curly" Lambeau, after whom our home field is named. The team is called the Packers because Lambeau was able to get the Indian Packing Company to agree to pay five hundred dollars for the team's uniforms—but only if Lambeau named the team after its sponsor.

Today the Packers are a publicly owned corporation, with more than a hundred thousand stockholders.

The Packers have featured some of the most famous players in NFL history, starting with Don Hutson, who led the league in receptions eight years in a row in the 1930s and

1940s. Then, after ten years of poor play, Lombardi took over the team in 1959, and with outstanding performers like Paul Hornung, Bart Starr, Jim Taylor, and Ray Nitschke, the Packers became America's Team, even though the Cowboys were so brazen as to call themselves that.

The Packers didn't win all that much in the 1970s and 1980s, but then in the 1990s quarterback Brett Favre and defensive lineman Reggie White came along to bring Green Bay renewed glory. In 1996 the Packers finished the season 13-3. After beating San Francisco in the mud and Carolina in freezing cold weather in the opening rounds of the playoffs, the Packers went to the Super Bowl for the first time in almost thirty years.

We defeated the New England Patriots 35–21. Desmond Howard returned a kickoff for a touchdown and was named MVP of the game.

When I joined the team in 1999 we had a new head coach, Ray Rhodes, a defensive specialist who had been coach of the Philadelphia Eagles. After losing to the San Francisco 49ers in a controversial playoff game in 1998, Mike Holmgren had quit and taken the job of head coach in Seattle. He took most of his staff with him.

When I arrived in Green Bay for the first time, I knew none of this. I knew only that Ron Wolf was the general manager, and I knew his name because he was the one who had called me to say the Packers had drafted me.

When I got off the plane, I was met by Packers football administrative coordinator Matt Klein. I should have been happy and grateful. I have to admit I came in feeling disrespected and pissed-off because I had been drafted so low.

In my first press conference, Sherman Lewis, the offensive coordinator, talked about me with faint praise.

"He'll go up in the crowd and come down with the ball," said Lewis. "But he's kind of a raw kid. If we take our time and bring him along slowly, a lot of times these guys develop."

It's not exactly what I wanted to hear. I wanted him to say I was going to start and be a star.

I was coming to a team with a ton of talent at quarterback. Besides Brett Favre we had three other excellent passers: Doug Pederson, Matt Hasselbeck, and Aaron Brooks.

How are all these guys going to play here? I wondered.

If I had had an adviser talk to me about the reality of my situation, I would have been asking the same question about myself.

When I reported, my locker wasn't even in the big room with the veterans. It was off to the side, and I even had to share it with another rookie, Zola Davis. When they assigned me uniform number 13, I asked whether I could have 3, my college number.

"No," I was told, "receivers in the NFL can't wear single digits."

I counted the wide receivers on the team. There was Jahine Arnold, Corey Bradford, Robert Brooks, Zola, Antonio Freeman, Tyrone Goodson, Desmond Howard, Derrick Mayes, Dee Miller, Bill Schroeder, Michael Vaughn, and Pat Palmer. I counted twelve competitors for the position.

And one more—me—number 13.

Are they telling me I'm not going to make the team? I wondered.

. . .

I WENT TO minicamp, a team practice in shorts and helmets before the real training camp, with everyone—rookies, free agents, tryout guys, and veterans—in attendance. Rookies had to dress early and be on the field first.

For a guy as self-confident as I was, this time I was nervous. Rookie camp wasn't a big deal. These were a bunch of guys coming in the same time I was, and all I had to do was look better than them. But when the veterans and free agents came in, the nerves started to get the best of me. Brett Favre was walking out onto that field, along with other guys whom I had watched when I was a kid.

Wow! I thought. *Now I can see these guys in person.*

When I walked on that field for the first time the first thing I did was get down on my knees and pray.

Okay, I told myself, *just have fun and try your hardest not to make any mistakes—and catch every ball that comes to you.*

And that's what I did. I was confident and nervous all at the same time, telling myself that all I had to do was do what I'd been doing since I was a little kid, and that was to have fun.

I worked and worked. I fought for every ball that was thrown, even if it was thrown out of bounds. I dove for everything and even ran into a fence a couple of times. I kept my frustration at being drafted so low to myself, and I came to work happy with a big smile on my face.

It was at the minicamp that I met Brett Favre for the first time.

We had a warm-up drill called "pad and go." The quarterback drops back, and the receivers take off and run. The purpose is merely to warm up your legs. Brett threw me a ball and I caught it. I was supposed to run to a different line for one of the other quarterbacks, but I wanted to make myself known to Brett, and so I ran the ball straight back to him and handed it to him.

"Hey, Donald, how ya doing?" he said.

I was elated.

"Don't worry," Brett said, "there are going to be plenty of those."

I was in awe. I was like a little kid. I had no idea how to act, and I probably made something of a fool of myself.

"You're awesome, awesome," I said to Brett. "I just caught a ball from you. *Yeah!*"

Brett looked at me like I was a little wacky. He didn't respond. I was hoping he believed in me, but I wasn't at all sure.

In the minicamp I found out there were two kinds of teammates: the ones who were focusing on saving their jobs and those who were there to help you. Among the helpers were Favre, and receivers Antonio Freeman, Bill Schroeder, and Robert Brooks, who became a close friend.

A couple of the other receivers went out of their way to try to make me look bad.

"Run this route," they'd tell me, and I'd run it, and it would be the wrong route. Early on I saw these guys weren't out to be a teammate, partner, or friend. They were doing what they could to get me tossed from the roster.

In the huddle one of these guys said to me, "Run a post."

I ran it when in fact I was supposed to run a hook. I came back to the huddle, and he was laughing.

"You should know you had a hook," he said.

I wanted to mash his face into a bloody pulp, but I was a rookie.

I can't trust these guys, I realized. I vowed I would study the playbook harder so I'd know exactly what I needed to do. All through training camp I studied like it was for a final exam.

CUT-DOWN DAY WAS traumatic. I was staying at the Midway Hotel along with the other rookies and first-year players. The Midway, an old hotel, is next to Lambeau Field. Training camp was over, and we were just waiting around to find out if we had made the team.

Most of us were waiting in the hallway. In my head I was trying to figure out who would stay and who would go, when I heard the phone ringing in my hotel room.

I ran to answer it. Reggie McKenzie, the Packers' director of personnel, was on the line.

My heart sank. I figured he was calling me with bad news.

"How are you doing, Drive?" he asked.

"I was doing good until you called," I said.

Reggie laughed.

"You had a good camp, Drive. The team likes you. You'll be a great fit."

"So what are you saying?"

"Congratulations," he said. "You made the roster. Now let me talk to your roommate."

I yelled for Zola Davis and told him he had a phone call.

"Who is it?" he asked.

I didn't have the heart to tell him. I handed him the phone and left the room.

When he hung up, I could see by his face that he had been cut. And he could see by mine that I had made it.

"How did *you* make the team?" he asked me.

I could only shrug.

"That sucks," he said.

Zola walked across the street to the stadium and handed in his playbook, and when he returned to our room I watched as he packed up all his belongings. I packed up mine, too, but I did it because I was moving into a new room with Tyrone Goodson, a receiver from Auburn who was hurt. Tyrone ended up on the practice squad.

A week before the first regular season game I was able to change my jersey from number 13 to number 80. Its previous owner, Derrick Mayes, went to Seattle, so it was available. Number 80, I felt, was perfect. My cousin Lawrence Driver and I both played high school ball and both of us loved Jerry Rice, who wore number 80 with San Francisco. We promised each other that if either of us made it to the NFL, he'd wear number 80. I would wear number 80 proudly for the next fourteen years.

CHAPTER 6

ROOKIE
BLUES

I BEGAN MY rookie year as the fifth receiver on the team. I was playing behind Antonio Freeman, Bill Schroeder, Corey Bradford, and Jaheen Arnold, whom the Packers had acquired from the Pittsburgh Steelers, but since I had started training camp as the thirteenth wide receiver on the team, I suppose I shouldn't have felt too bad about not starting.

Early in the season I could see I wasn't in the plans of head coach Ray Rhodes, at least not yet, but I never got down on myself, because of the praise I was getting from Packers general manager Ron Wolf. I never would have made the Packers without him. His faith in me pushed me every single day. I would see him while I was on the practice field. He wore a wide-brimmed hat and dark sunglasses, and he'd stand with his hands folded across his chest, usually talking to a scout or one of the veteran players. He was close to Antonio Freeman, Reggie White, and Sean Jones, and I would look over to where he was standing and say to myself, *I cannot let this guy down. He's done so much for me. I have to make this guy proud.* At the same time I couldn't wait for the day when I could stand and talk with him without the pressure of having to make the team.

At the end of my first week of practice Ron sent an assistant to the locker room to get me.

"Ron wants to see you in his office," I was told.

I couldn't imagine what that was all about.

"I wanted to congratulate you," he said. "And I have something for you. Follow me."

We walked from his office in Lambeau Field down to the Packers Pro Shop store.

I thought perhaps I'd find my jersey with the number 80 on the back being sold.

"Do you own anything with Packers on it?" he asked.

I had the team-issued practice and workout gear, but it wasn't mine. I couldn't take it home.

I had to admit I didn't.

Ron and I walked around the store, looking at different items, checking out the prices.

"I'm going to let him pick out anything in the store," he told the salesclerk.

I wasn't used to people buying me presents.

Anything? I wondered. *As many as I want?*

I was told I could pick any one item.

"Anything you want," he said, and he turned to go, leaving me to decide.

"Thank you, Mr. Wolf," I said.

As he walked out the door he waved me off.

I walked around the store feeling as happy as a person could feel. I looked at everything. There were replica jerseys of Brett Favre, Dorsey Levens, Reggie White, and Antonio Freeman. I considered buying a Favre or White jersey and having the player sign it for me. But fall in Wisconsin was coming soon, and I didn't have a winter coat. On a rack was a baseball-style, black leather jacket with a big Packer *G* on the front. I couldn't help staring at it. I thought it was awesome.

I was concerned that the price, three hundred dollars, would be excessive, but Mr. Wolf did say I could pick out anything I wanted, and I really wanted that jacket. I didn't have any status, and I figured if I wore that coat downtown, people would know I played for the Packers. I wanted to be somebody. I wanted people to notice me.

I was such a rookie. Later Antonio Freeman would tell me, "You don't have to do that. People will know you play for the Packers." And of course he was right about that.

My mom has that jacket now. It was from a guy who believed in me. If I should ever get inducted into the Hall of Fame, and if we're both alive, Ron Wolf will be there to induct me, and I will wear that jacket.

"Don't ever get rid of that leather jacket," I told my mom.

It's still sitting up in my room at home.

UPON MY ARRIVAL in Green Bay I made a vow to myself that I would embrace every moment. I would also embrace the fans. I had heard some guys described as jerks by fans, and I didn't want to be one of those players. My rookie year I was a nobody. My jersey wasn't even in stores. But after training camp practice or minicamp practice I would stand outside and sign autographs for hours just to show the fans I loved them. Things work in mysterious ways, because to this day you see the love and support that the fans have given me and that has to be because of the love and support I showed them through those early years of my career.

When I joined the Packers I had no idea about the magical history of the franchise. As I said, I didn't even know where Green Bay was. I didn't know about Vince Lombardi, Bart Starr, Paul Hornung, and the other Packer greats when I arrived in town. I had no idea of the excitement I was about to be involved in until I played in the Family Night scrimmage at Lambeau Field.

The offense was to scrimmage against the defense. It didn't seem like any big deal to me. As I walked out the old tunnel that all the Packers of the past had walked through, I was standing next to Brett Favre. I didn't know what to expect.

"This ain't Alcorn State University," Brett said to me. "This ain't seventeen thousand people. Tonight there are going to be fifty-five thousand people in the stands."

I thought he was crazy.

"No way there are going to be fifty-five thousand fans," I said. "For a scrimmage?"

I walked out of that little tunnel, and I looked up and heard the roar, and I could see that the stadium was jam-packed with the Green Bay faithful. That's when I said to myself, *This place is special. I'm not in Mississippi anymore.*

When I joined the Packers I joined a team that had just seen legendary Reggie White retire. Reggie had a great work ethic that was well documented. I would see him from time to time, and what I learned from him was invaluable.

"The way you practice," he told me, "is the way you're

going to play the game. You can't take time off. Give it your all—every play."

And that's exactly what Reggie would do. There were actually times when I would look around and say to myself, *I'm playing on the same field that Reggie White, one of the greatest players of all time, played on.*

Reggie held the title of Minister of Defense. Guys who played with him said he was a minister in the locker room. He didn't like people to cuss around him. He was a Christian man, and I'd heard that if anyone in the locker room did anything wrong, he'd be the first to come over and say, "You can't do that. It's not that I don't approve of it. God doesn't approve of it."

My rookie year he came up to me once and said, "Drive, you're going to be a superstar one day. You just keep working."

I have never forgotten his kindness.

Reggie died in his sleep in late December 2004 at age forty-three. The year before he died I asked him to sign a jersey for me. He called me Hammer. I don't know why. Maybe he got it from the old saying that it's better to be a hammer than a nail. Maybe he thought I looked like M. C. Hammer. He signed the jersey, "To Donald Hammer, Reggie White." It was the last time we ever spoke. I still have the jersey hanging on my wall at home.

One Packer I loved to practice against was cornerback Mike McKenzie. He was a third-round pick out of Memphis the same year I was drafted. He had dreadlocks and a swagger about him that said, *I'm one of the best defensive backs in the whole world.* I'd practice against him every day, one-on-one. It's one of the reasons I improved as quickly as I did.

Mike was an interesting cat. He didn't try to get to know anyone. He didn't come up to you and say, "I want to be your friend." You had to earn his friendship. And I did that. Mike and I talk to this day. He and I both know who our true friends are.

I WAS ECSTATIC when I made the team, but the thrill wore off quickly when I didn't play in the first nine games of the 1999 season. I didn't even travel. I had to watch the Packers road games from my home.

My rookie season in Green Bay was Tina's senior year at Alcorn. I had to go to Green Bay by myself. I was making decent money for the first time in my life, $125,000 a year, and I found a nice duplex apartment in De Pere, Wisconsin, that I rented for $875 a month.

Tina was back at school, and she was nervous because I was gone. The first thing she said to me after I arrived at camp was "You're going to leave me and go out and find a white girl to marry. It's what you guys [football players] do."

I started laughing. She was so funny.

"Tina," I said, "I'm *not* going to find a white girl to marry. I love you. I promise I love you, and I'm going to be good."

We laugh about it to this day. I think what she was most nervous about was that I was going to be away from her. And in truth many athletes do leave and do find another girl to marry, leaving behind their college sweethearts. So her worries were understandable. I don't know what made her say "white girl" but she said it, and I told her, "We're going to be together forever."

That first year in Green Bay I was very lonely without her. The first nine games I wasn't playing, and I missed her and wanted to see her, so I would fly her up every other weekend. Right after practice on Friday I would drive three and a half hours to Chicago and pick her up at around 1 P.M., and I'd drive back to Green Bay. We'd spend the weekend together, and then on Monday or Tuesday I'd drive her back to Chicago.

She would cry. I would cry. We had a lot of love for each other, and we missed each other.

We got married the following March, and after the ceremony she moved straight to Green Bay.

WHEN WE PLAYED at Lambeau that 1999 season, I stood on the sidelines in street clothes and watched. Even so, the whole time I worked hard to win over Brett Favre whenever I could. In practice he threw to the starters, and I worked with one of the backup quarterbacks, Matt Hasselbeck, Doug Pederson, or Aaron Brooks, but then after practice the starters would leave and Brett would stay behind to throw to rookie receiver Corey Bradford and me. Brett could throw rockets, and we needed to get used to catching his throws. I'm sure Brett just wanted to see if we could catch his fastballs. Corey preferred catching with his body. I always caught with my hands.

NFL football is brutal, and I knew it was only a matter of time before someone got hurt, and I would get to play.

The opportunity came in the tenth game of the season, against the Dallas Cowboys, a great defensive team led by Deion Sanders at cornerback. Not only did Corey and I dress for the game, but the coaches even put in a special play for us. They called it the SWAC package, because I had played at Alcorn State and Corey had played at Jackson State, and both schools were in the Southwest Athletic Conference.

On the second play of the game, we went into the huddle and Brett called the SWAC package. As you might have guessed, the play called for us to run down the sidelines as fast as we could and head for daylight.

Corey ran down the right sideline, and I ran down the left. Corey beat Deion, and he beat him down the field, and Brett hit Corey right in the hands. But as he ran to catch the ball, he popped a hamstring. The ball fell to the ground, as did Corey.

I was a rookie playing my first NFL game, and not knowing any better, I ran over to see if Corey was okay. Meanwhile, the coaches on the sideline were screaming at me, "Donald, get in the game!"

I didn't know what to do. My friend was lying there in pain. I ran back to the huddle just lost. I kept running routes, but I was frustrated because Favre wasn't looking for me.

We had the ball trailing Dallas 20–13 with little time left. There were three plays left. The ball was snapped, and I ran down the left sideline. Deion, perhaps sensing I wasn't going to get the ball no matter how open I was, didn't chase. I was wide open. I waved my hands, and Brett threw the ball.

I dove to make the catch, and I was excited because I

was sure I had scored a touchdown. But when I looked up, I realized I was fifty feet out of bounds.

I've got to be nuts, I thought.

On the next play Antonio Freeman and I switched positions. He was in the slot and I went wide. Dallas was playing a zone, and Freeman ran to a seam. Brett threw him the ball, and Dallas safety George Teague intercepted it and ran it ninety-five yards for a touchdown to seal the Dallas win.

My brother Moses came to the game, and he was ecstatic.

"You beat Deion Sanders. Oh yeah," he said.

I had yet to catch a single pass in the NFL.

That day came in our fourteenth game of the season, against the Carolina Panthers at home. I got to play because Corey Bradford had suffered a concussion and wasn't able to play. I made three key catches that day, two on third down to move the chains, and an eight-yard touchdown pass. Brett called "two jet flanker drive," and I went in motion, ran across the field, and got myself wide open. Brett threw it, I caught it at the one-yard line, and I made a little move to get into the end zone.

I started to do my own little dance, something I had learned on the dance floor. I was so raw I didn't know about the Lambeau Leap—a Packer player celebrates catching a touchdown by leaping into the stands. It was started by LeRoy Butler years before and has been copied by players all over the league. Don't be fooled, though. The only legitimate Lambeau Leap is celebrated by a Packer at Lambeau Field.

When I returned to the bench Antonio Freeman was all over me.

"What are you doing?" he said. "What was that? Next time you score a touchdown, jump into the stands."

I told him I'd do the Lambeau Leap the next time I scored at home.

That would not happen for another two years.

CHAPTER 7

A NEW REGIME

MY HEAD COACH my rookie season was Ray Rhodes, who in his first year coaching the Philadelphia Eagles was named NFL Coach of the Year. Three seasons later Ray was fired. When Mike Holmgren left the Packers to become head coach and general manager of the Seattle Seahawks in 1998, GM Ron Wolf chose Ray. He was the only candidate to interview for the position.

Wolf chose Ray because he was player-friendly, and that was his way. It seemed that Ray spent more time playing cards or dominoes in the locker room with the players than he did upstairs with the front office and the rest of the coaching staff. His offensive coordinator, Sherman Lewis, was also a players' coach. Sherman called the best plays. He put the right players in the right place to win. He would laugh and joke with the guys all the time. If I had a son and had to pick a coach for him to play for, I would pick Sherman Lewis. But like Ray Rhodes, he was friends with the players, and often when you do that, the players end up taking advantage.

Ray would say, "I should not have to come in and force you guys to work. I should not have to make you want to win games."

Some players need to be motivated by a tough taskmaster. Some players need to have the fear of God to make them play hard. I do think Ray became so attached to the players that he wasn't the disciplinarian he needed to be. Ray was our buddy, and the players took advantage.

Ironically, it was Ray Rhodes who taught me an important lesson. We were in Chicago. Corey Bradford and I were roommates. We got off the elevator to go to a special teams meeting, and we ran into Ray.

He looked at us and tapped his watch.

"You guys are late," he said.

"No, we have five minutes," I said.

"Not by my watch," he said. "You guys are late. You owe me."

He fined each of us five hundred dollars. For a rookie, that's a lot of money.

Corey argued with him.

"Aw, come on . . ."

It didn't work. We were fined. And after that I was always early. I never was fined again, at least off the field.

By the end of the season Ron Wolf could see that the Packers weren't playing up to our potential. After losing close games to Carolina and Minnesota, we were beaten badly by Tampa Bay before winning our final game against Arizona to finish the season a mediocre 8-8.

Ron Wolf had seen enough after one season, and Ray and his entire staff were fired.

For me it was like starting all over again.

• • •

In 2000 I was invited to qualify again for the Olympics in the high jump. At Alcorn State I had jumped seven feet, five inches, and I had a very good shot at winning a medal.

When I returned to Green Bay to begin training for my second season, I went to see Ron Wolf and tell him of my opportunity.

He was blunt.

"You have to make a decision," he said. "Either run track or play football."

To get ready for the Olympics I would have to miss the rest of camp and the start of the 2000 season. Making things more difficult was that our new coach, Mike Sherman, didn't know me from Adam. I could see that if I left to train for the Olympics, Ron Wolf would have said, "Nice medal. Pack your stuff."

I decided the smart move was to stick with football.

Mike Sherman was a whole lot different from Ray Rhodes. Mike, a no-nonsense martinet, had no interest in being our buddies. He also had no respect for rookies, and though this was my second year, I was treated as a rookie. He felt that rookies didn't know enough to have an opinion, and he gave the impression that rookies had no right to say anything. His attitude: They shouldn't come to me and ask things; they shouldn't question why we do the things we do around here.

If a rookie had a suggestion or a comment, he would cut him off.

"You should practice," he would say. "That's all you do."

Under Mike the practices were grueling, and that included training camp, when we had two-a-days. We were in pads the first six practices. That meant all-out hitting. We spent a morning in pads, an afternoon in pads, a morning in pads, another afternoon in pads, a third morning in pads, and another afternoon in pads. Hitting, hitting, hitting all day. As I said, it was grueling.

Mike drew boundaries. Unlike Ray Rhodes, who allowed the coaches to play cards with the players, Mike insisted the coaches stay with the coaches, and the players stay with the players. He insisted, and he was not going to change for anyone.

He called me into his office.

"I don't care what you did your rookie year," he said. "You're going to have to make this squad playing on the special teams."

It was as though I was starting over.

I wasn't happy about it, but I decided that if I was going to be on the special teams, I was going to be the best special teams player I could be.

My job was to be the gunner. Whenever the Packers punted the ball, my job was to run down the field, avoid the two defenders trying to stop me, and go nose-to-nose with the punt returner so that if he did anything but signal for a fair catch, I would plant him into the ground.

I confess: I was so mad I couldn't be a wide receiver that any time I had the chance to nail the punt returner, I took full advantage of it.

When we were doing the punting, my other job was to be a jammer. I was to find the other team's top gunner and stop him from getting to one of our punt returners: Desmond Howard, Antonio Freeman, Allen Rossum, or Antonio Chatman.

I did my job well. In a preseason game against the New York Jets, the Jets kicked off to us, and on the very first play I knocked the Jets' gunner completely off his feet.

When I returned to the sidelines special teams coach Frank Novak said to me, "Congratulations, Drive. You've made this team."

I would be named the alternate on special teams for the Pro Bowl.

I REALLY LIKED Mike Sherman, our new head coach. I'd say he was hugely responsible for my becoming the player I became. When he walked into Green Bay in 2000, he literally didn't know who I was.

"Where did you come from?" he asked me.

"Alcorn State," I said with a smile, "a small school in the state of Mississippi."

"Continue to work," he said. It was his mantra. Often when he saw me he would repeat, "Continue to work."

I went out every day and worked as hard as I could.

During my early years as a Packer, it seemed, I was always "on the bubble." In other words, I wasn't a sure thing. I was on the bubble during training camp to make the roster, then on the bubble to start, and later I'd be on the bubble to become a receiver. Nothing, it seemed, was ever given to me.

I'd even say to Sherman, "You know, I'm on the bubble."

"As long as you play this game," he would say, "you'll be on the bubble."

And looking back I can see how right he was. As long as

you're playing professional football, no matter how well you're doing, you are *always* on the bubble.

Mike Sherman kept to himself unless he chose to get to know you. If he wanted a relationship with a player, it was up to him to initiate it. That's how it was with me. During my first two years, he kept me at arm's length. Things changed in 2002 when I became a starting receiver.

Going into training that year I wasn't under consideration for that role. The Packers had acquired Terry Glenn from the New England Patriots, and they made Javon Walker out of Florida State the twentieth pick of the draft. Robert Ferguson from Texas A&M was drafted in the second round and was another choice. And then there was me.

Glenn was acquired from the Patriots for two fourth-round draft picks; he was traded because he missed most of the 2001 season with injuries and because he couldn't get along with Patriots coach Bill Belichick. He went public with an admission that he was faking an injury because Belichick was too rough on his players. After the Patriots won the Super Bowl, they mailed him his ring instead of giving it to him personally.

Mike knew my goal was to start as a wide receiver, and he personally taught me how to play the position. He taught me the X's and O's. He taught me what to look for in the defense. When I finally began playing wide receiver in 2001 he would pull me aside and explain why he switched a route or why he wanted me to run the route he chose.

"Why can't I run it another way?" I would ask, and he would explain in great detail that the opposition was scheming to take away a particular route, and if I did it my way, I would be stopped. It was like I was taking a graduate course in Understanding Offensive Football. You don't normally get that kind of attention from a head coach.

Mike would always tell me, "Drive, don't be so fast running your routes. Relax. Be patient."

"I'm always patient," I'd say, and he'd argue with me.

"That's the nuts side of you," he'd say. "You *think* you're being patient, but you're really not."

He taught me the concepts, and he taught me how to focus. His lessons stayed with me my entire career, long after he had left Green Bay.

TWO TEAMMATES, OUR star halfback Ahman Green, who came to the Packers from the University of Nebraska, and Marco Rivera, a guard out of Penn State, left an impression on me because of their ability to play practical jokes. One day Marco decided he was going to play a practical joke on Ahman. He went to a pet store and bought a bag full of live crickets, then threw the chirpy little creatures into the cab of Ahman's truck. Ahman always had cool cars with nice wheels.

Ahman got in his truck, and before he could even turn on the ignition, he heard the crickets. He turned around to look where the noise was coming from. His truck was crawling with noisy insects.

Ahman jumped out, totally freaked out. Of course, he knew immediately who was responsible.

The next day Ahman decided to get back at Marco. He hired a tow truck to lift Marco's Hummer off the ground, take the wheels off, and put it on blocks in the middle of the Lambeau Field parking lot.

Marco couldn't drive it for about a week.

The prank is still talked about in the Packers locker room.

After watching them, I thought, *I'm not going to mess with either of those guys.* When it came to pranks, those guys were professionals.

THROUGH MINICAMPS AND the training camps I continued to develop my relationship with Brett Favre. We developed a chemistry.

Throughout training camp in 2002 Javon Walker struggled to catch the ball, and Bob Ferguson had back problems that limited his playing time. Terry Glenn played well, and so did I.

As the season was getting under way receivers coach Ray Sherman told us they had changed their minds. The starting receivers were going to be Terry Glenn and me. All that hard work had paid off.

The Packers were an excellent, well-disciplined team in 2002. Our record during the regular season was 12-4, the Packers' best since 1997. We finished first in the NFC North division. We went 8-1 in our first nine games. Brett Favre was brilliant.

After beating Atlanta and Detroit and losing to New Orleans, we played the Carolina Panthers at Lambeau in late September. In that game I made Mike Sherman proud when I caught two touchdowns for 97 yards. Mike had told the press that one of his goals in 2002 was to improve the speed of his receivers, and with Terry and me now starting, he had accomplished that goal. My first touchdown reception didn't come from Brett but rather from tight end Bubba Franks. I started the play like I was blocking, and then I took off downfield. Bubba went out like he was running a reverse, Brett tossed the ball to him behind the line of scrimmage, and Bubba deftly threw it to me in the corner of the end zone.

Then I caught a Favre pass over the middle to win the game 17–14. I jumped up and caught the ball just as the defender grabbed my face mask and twisted my helmet over my face. I was fixing my helmet as I ran into the end zone.

Four games later, against Detroit, I caught eleven passes for 130 yards and a touchdown in a 40–14 win. In a rare loss, this one 31–21 to Minnesota, I caught four passes for 120 yards, including an 84-yard catch-and-run up the left sideline for a touchdown.

The play, which tied the score at 21, was called a Double Winston.

"If the safety stays back," Brett said to me in the huddle, "I'm going to hit you in the hole."

Terry Glenn ran the pivot—a route where he ran the seven yards and just stopped. He attracted a linebacker and a corner, leaving the middle of the field open. I filled that hole, and Brett hit me. I made the safety miss, and I took off running. Terry ran next to me. When I scored I was so happy, I threw the ball up into the stands and was running so fast I continued into the end zone tunnel.

I had my breakout year with 70 catches and 1,064 yards in 2002. I led the Packers in receiving and earned my first visit to the Pro Bowl. For the first time in a long time the Packers had a realistic chance of reaching the Super Bowl.

AT THE END of the 2001 season I could have become an unrestricted free agent. In fact the Kansas City Chiefs had let me know that they were willing to give me a three-year deal for $3 million with a $695,000 signing bonus if I signed with them when my contract ran out.

At this time Tina and I were looking to buy a house in the Green Bay area.

"Babe," I told her, "we're not sure we're going to be here."

"We're going to be here," Tina said. "I want a house. I'm tired of living in an apartment."

I don't know what I was thinking, but we ended up buying the house Tina wanted. I signed a one-year deal with Green Bay for $695,000, which was nothing to sneeze at.

During the 2002 season the Packers offered me a couple of long-term contracts, including one for five years for $8 million, but Tina was adamant that they weren't offering me enough, and so I turned them down. I kept telling her, "We need to sign a deal soon, because you never know what's going to happen."

After week nine against Chicago, Mike Sherman pulled me into his office and offered me a five-year, $11.5 million contract.

"Now you'll be able to take care of your family," he said.

Tina still felt I could get more, but this time I felt it was too risky to turn it down.

"They're offering a nice contract with a nice bonus," I told her. "It's a long season. You never know. I don't think we should turn this money down."

I didn't have a lot of money like some players. I wasn't a first-round draft choice. Tina finally agreed the offer was good enough, and I signed it in November 2002.

And it was a good thing I did. I was hurt in the final game of the season. Had I not signed, I know what they would have said: "He's not as valuable anymore."

The final game of the 2002 season was against the New York Jets. Our record was 12-3 when we played them, and we were trounced 42–17, costing Brett the MVP trophy. The Oakland Raiders' Rich Gannon would beat him out by only two votes.

Early in the Jets game I ran a reverse. I took the ball from Brett behind the line of scrimmage and tried to make a move, but the Jets defense had me covered. Instead of sliding to avoid injury, I put my arm on the ground just when I was hit. In lay terms I had a badly separated shoulder. In medical speak my acromioclavicular joint popped out of my right shoulder. The trauma to the shoulder damaged the ligaments holding the two shoulder bones—the scapula and the clavicle—together.

As I lay on the ground, I couldn't move my arm. It felt as though someone had stuck the blade of a knife into my shoulder. I was in agony.

As Packers assistant trainer Kurt Fielding escorted me to the locker room, he kept asking me how I felt. My shoulder hurt so bad I was on the verge of tears. I went home on the plane with my arm in a sling.

Even though our record was 12-4, we didn't have a first-round bye in the playoffs. We had to play the Atlanta Falcons, with only a week to prepare.

It was devastating to think I wouldn't be able to participate in the playoff game against the Falcons.

"I *have* to play," I told team physician Dr. Patrick McKenzie.

Despite the intense pain I decided to fight the agony and return to the field no matter what. I had just signed a big deal. I didn't want to let anyone down. And when you're hurt, management starts to think that you're injury-prone.

Not too many players would have played through the injuries I had over the years. I played through quad injuries, neck injuries, and shoulder injuries, and almost never missed a game. In fifteen years I missed three games, and two of those were because of injuries. Dr. McKenzie said that no one else would have ever done that.

"Donald," he once told me, "you're a different breed than most players."

For me it was a point of pride.

During the early part of the week I didn't practice. Coach Sherman let me know that if I couldn't practice, I wouldn't be able to play in the game. The Friday before the game was my last chance to get out on the field.

Friday's practice was short, and I knew that all I had to do was show them I could play. Coach Sherman had me wear shoulder pads just to make sure I could move my shoulder in them.

I pulled Brett aside.

"Everything needs to be low," I told him. "All the passes

have to be at my chest or lower. I can't reach anything over my head."

All practice long Brett threw balls low, and I caught everything. I caught the balls near my chest, and I even got one just below my chin. Brett then called for what we call a hammer route. I ran across the field, and Brett let it fly. The ball was up, but football is a game of instinct, and I reached up, forgetting that my shoulder was damaged. I stretched my arm way over my head, grabbed the ball, and came crashing down to earth in terrible, terrible pain.

"That's it for me today," I told receivers coach Ray Sherman.

"What's wrong?"

"My shoulder."

I knew Ray intended to tell Mike Sherman, and I knew that if he did that, Mike wouldn't let me play in the play-off game. I pleaded with Ray to tell Mike that I had caught enough, had showed them I could do it, and that I should sit out the rest of practice. I told Brett the same thing.

I sat on the bench as though everything were fine, but I was in agonizing pain. My shoulder was screaming, and there was nothing I could do. My joint was up in the air, and the doctor could fix it only if I returned to the locker room, which I finally was able to do at the end of practice.

In the trainer's room I whispered that I'd need help getting off the pads. Mike Sherman never did know.

On Saturday I pleaded with Dr. McKenzie to give me a painkiller. He tested me for strength and power, and I passed all the tests. My only problem was the pain I was suffering, and he didn't like giving painkillers unless he absolutely had to.

He put me off.

I kept at him Saturday night, and finally he agreed to give me a shot just before the game.

I'd guess you probably don't understand why it was so important for me to play, considering the pain I was in. I had signed a new five-year contract before the season, and I felt I owed it to the team and to the Green Bay fans. But more important, I was a competitor and all my life I had treated important games like they were a matter of life and death.

I've just had an amazing year, I told myself. *I have to play.*

I went out for the pregame warm-ups in my pads. I didn't catch anything high. If the ball came to me over my pads, I'd let it sail over my head, looking at Brett as if to say, *You don't expect me to catch that, do you?*

After warm-ups I hopped up on the table ready for my shot.

Doc showed me where it was going to go, and he marked the spot with a blue marker.

"Are you ready?" he asked. "Take a deep breath."

"Hold on," I said. "Let me see it first."

The needle was a good six inches long. I shivered.

"You'll be fine," Doc reassured me. "I won't put it all the way in, just enough to get the medicine in there."

Doc injected the medicine. My eyes were pinched shut. The shot hurt.

And then—no pain.

I felt like I had conquered the world.

I could play.

I played in the first half against the Falcons and did just

fine. But there is only so much a shot can do. Brett threw me a deep ball down the middle of the field on a slant route. I jumped up and made the catch, and then I landed on my bad shoulder. I was in agony.

My face was planted in the grass and I was gasping for air. Brett ran over to me.

"Get up," he screamed. "Get up right now! I need you. Get up!"

Somehow I rose and walked to the sidelines.

"I don't think you can go anymore," said receivers coach Ray Sherman. "I think you're done."

Even though I couldn't raise my shoulder and was in terrible pain, I told Ray, "No, no, no. I've got to play. Brett needs me. He needs me."

I went over to Doc and told him, "It's dead now. You've got to shoot it again."

We went to the locker room. I again needed help getting off my shoulder pads. Doc gave me another shot—it went into the same spot, but this time the pain of the shot was so great I almost flipped off the table.

I can't let Brett and the rest of the team down, was all I could think of. I ran back onto Lambeau Field. The crowd let out a roar, motivating me to keep fighting through the pain.

Let's play, baby. Let's play.

I dove and caught another ball, again landing on my shoulder, but I stayed in the game. On the first drive of the second half I caught the lone Packers touchdown, a fourteen-yard pass from Brett. I lay in the end zone, thinking, *This is it.* I knew my shoulder wasn't going to give me anything more.

I came off the field. Doc pushed down on the acromio-clavicular joint and told me, "You're done."

I wouldn't hear of it.

Only I decide when I'm done, I told myself, *and I'm not leaving this game.*

I was standing on the sidelines, and I looked down at Brett. We were on the way to a 27–7 loss, and at this point Brett didn't think it was worth it for me to continue. He shook his head. When he did that, that's when I knew I was done for the day. I walked off the field brokenhearted.

Before our loss to Michael Vick and the Falcons, the Packers had never lost a playoff game at Lambeau Field. To be part of the first team ever to lose at Lambeau was tough.

It was the first time we were ever booed by Packers fans.

CHAPTER 8

PERSEVERANCE

I DIDN'T WANT to leave the Packers. Mike Sherman had schooled me in the art of pass catching, and he had been the one to showcase my talents enough for another team to even want me. I felt I owed him and the Packers my loyalty and gratitude, and in November 2002, when I signed a five-year extension with the Packers, I was happy I'd be able to call Green Bay my home.

At my press conference I thought back to when my brother Moses was in the third grade and I was in the second. We were lying in our bed in an apartment building in Houston. My mom was married to Sam at the time. Tamela and Trice were in their room sleeping, and as I lay there, I said to Moses, "I'm going to take our family out of this one day. We're not going to struggle like we're struggling now. We're not going to live check to check. We're going to have a better life."

My brother laughed.

"I hope that's true," he said.

And then all of a sudden it came true.

I HAVE ALWAYS wanted to help others, as others have helped me along the way, and I started doing charity work when I first hit Green Bay in 1999. My intention was that if I ever made it to the National Football League, my status as a pro football player would provide the perfect platform for me to raise money for various charities. After having been homeless when I was a boy, I felt it was important for me to now give back to the community, both in Green Bay and in Texas.

I started doing appearances. Sometimes they paid me, but many of them were for free, and between 1999 and 2002 I made some three hundred of them.

I've been a spokesman for the United Way; the Salvation Army; the Juvenile Diabetes Research Foundation; the Special Olympics; Big Brothers, Big Sisters; and numerous other charities. I've hosted an Evening of Elegance, golf outings, football camps, and other events to help the less fortunate.

In 2003 Goodwill Industries asked me to do an appearance for them. The ad campaign was called "The Power of Partners," and after that appearance, they asked me to come back again. Because of my background and my visibility as a Packer, they thought I made a good spokesman. They felt I fit in well with their "Power of Work" slogan, and they knew I'd support the idea of giving people with disabilities an opportunity.

I have met so many wonderful people with disabilities through Goodwill. I asked to go to their warehouse in Milwaukee, and I met and greeted people in wheelchairs, people with Down syndrome, amputees—and what I loved most about them was that though they didn't have all the tools, it didn't change who they were. They were some of the happiest people I ever met. They were living their lives, saying, *It's okay. I'm okay with this.* They wanted hugs. They wanted to

talk. They wanted to take pictures. They said they were surprised I was so down to earth.

"I'm just like you," I said. "I'm no better than you are."

Sometimes I think about what would happen to me if I
lost an arm or a leg. What if I were in a wheelchair? Would
I be the same person? After meeting the people at Goodwill,
I think maybe I would be okay with it, just as they were.

I did the first Goodwill ad by myself. After that, I decided
I should do them with my family because Goodwill is all about
bringing families together. Almost every commercial I've done
for them has been with my family. There's one commercial in
which Tina, my son, Cristian, and I sit in a park talking about
the power of work. I was so happy Goodwill allowed me to be
part of their family. Others gave me the opportunity to better
my life, and it was easy for me to get on board with Goodwill.

I am also proud of my association with the Wisconsin
Department of Transportation, doing public service announce-
ments to encourage people to buckle up their seat belts when
they travel in their cars.

When I first started doing the commercials, I'm embarrassed to say, I didn't use my seat belt very often. And then a
friend of mine, Ashley Knetzger, a nineteen-year-old waitress at
the Texas Roadhouse on Oneida Street in Green Bay, was killed
in a terrible accident in which a speeding car ran a red light
and killed her and her friend. Neither of them was wearing a
seat belt. I doubt they'd have survived even with a seat belt, but
from that day on I resolved never to drive without wearing one.

I tell that story when I do the DOT spots. I also encourage parents to install their children's safety seats the proper

way. Now when I get in the car, before I turn on the ignition I make sure Tina and the kids are buckled up.

Tina and I do most of our charily work through the Donald Driver Foundation, which raises money for homeless families to pay rent and move into a home. We started our foundation in 2000, as a private foundation funded through my salary.

One afternoon I was talking with Andre Credit, my quarterback at Alcorn and a close friend of mine, and he said, "Donald, you need to open this up to become a public foundation, so you can get donations from different companies."

"What are you talking about?" I asked him.

"Host a golf tournament," he said.

"I don't care for that," I told him. "I just want to give the foundation money from my pocket so I can make sure the money goes out to the community."

"That's what public charities do," he said. "You ask the community to give you money, and you donate it all back."

When I sat down with my accountant, he said the same thing.

"You need to make it a public foundation," he told me.

In 2002 we transformed it into a public foundation, and we started raising money to feed homeless families, support education, and do cancer research.

Our foundation also has helped more than a thousand families feed their children on the weekend through our "Blessings in Backpack" program. Children on welfare get a free school lunch, but too often they have nothing to eat on the weekends. We ask people to donate eighty dollars to help feed these kids on the weekends.

To help raise money for these and other charities, I hold a softball game, which I took over after Brett Favre retired. In 2013 it took place for the sixth consecutive year. The last two years the game has been sold out, I am proud to say.

We've had a great time doing it, and we've raised a lot of money. I am looking forward to raising a lot more in the future. In 2013, I was honored with the AMVETS National Ladies Humanitarian Award—but for me, the real joy comes in just impacting lives.

AT MY PRESS conference to announce my new contract, through nervous trembling, tears, and a couple of loud sobs, I told those in attendance: "I never thought I'd get the opportunity to take care of my family. I have that opportunity now."

I thanked Mike Sherman, team vice president Andrew Brandt, and my agent Jordan Woy for getting the deal done.

"I never wanted to leave Green Bay," I said. "I've always said I wanted to stay and have the opportunity to retire as a Green Bay Packer."

When I said, "When I talked to my grandmother, it was just so surprising I could tell her, 'You don't have to work anymore,'" I was sobbing.

When I finally made it in football, I realized that I had an obligation to take care of my entire family. My grandparents never asked for much, but I wanted to make sure they were comfortable and had cars to drive, and so I paid off their house and cars. If they have bills, they know they can always pick up the phone assured that I will make their day, knowing I would never deny them. It puts a smile on my face to know I've made them happy.

My mom and Tina's mom will never have to work another day in their lives.

"You guys are set for life," is what I told them. "You will never have to do anything."

"You raised me all your life," I told my mom. "Now it's time for me to help you live your life."

During the whole time I played pro football I gave all four of my brothers and sisters—Tamela, Moses, Patrice, and Sam Jr.—monthly stipends to allow them to live comfortably. My sister Tamela is doing well. She's going back to school. She has five kids and grandkids. My brother has a beautiful wife and two beautiful kids. His wife is a pharmacist at Walgreens. His kids go to school.

Trice is working. She has a job, and she's happy and living every day to the fullest. Sam loves horses, just like his dad. He's a country boy who loves to rope bulls and ride horses.

All five of us siblings have a bond that will never go away.

"This money is not just mine," I told my family, my grandparents, my mom, and my brothers and sisters. "It's all of ours. We're not going to spend it like money grows on trees. We're going to do it in a positive way so none of us will ever have to struggle again."

THE YEAR 2002 was also the year I became a father. For the longest time, because of my upbringing—the homelessness, the moving around, the changing father figures—I was more afraid of fatherhood than anything else. I didn't want kids of mine to have to go through what I went through. I never wanted a child of mine to worry about where his or her next meal was coming from. Or where he or she was going to lay his or her head. Or whether the lights or gas would go on.

When we were first married, I told Tina I didn't want to have kids.

"I don't want to live check to check," I said. "I don't want a collection agency coming through my home and taking all my belongings. I'd rather you and I go through that than any kids."

"Maybe one day you'll change your mind," she said.

When I had enough confidence that no longer would we have to worry about paying the bills, I told Tina I was on board with fatherhood.

In March 2002 we were going out to celebrate our second wedding anniversary when Tina announced she was pregnant. I was elated. We told friends and family the good news.

Not long afterward Tina had to use the restroom. I could hear her scream. I went inside, and there was blood everywhere. I rushed her to the hospital. She had miscarried. She lay in her hospital bed sobbing.

I was hurting just as badly. I closed the door of the bathroom in her hospital room, giving myself the privacy to grieve and to let the tears flow. But I also knew I had to be strong for Tina, and when I emerged, I walked back to Tina and told her, "It's going to be okay. The good thing is, we can still have kids. We're blessed."

I took her home that night, but she was suffering from a deep depression. I went out to participate in off-season workouts, and when I returned she was still in bed. It took a few days for her to rebound. I was glad this happened in the off-season, when I could be home with her.

We had to wait six weeks before we could try again.

Before one of the Packers home games in October 2002, I was staying over in the team hotel. Mike Sherman made us do this, because he knew if he didn't, we would be bombarded by friends and family who wanted tickets or dinner reservations or something else that would take our minds off the game at hand. Trying to entertain guests can be exhausting, enough so that the game itself feels like a Christmas holiday from the stadium tours, taking everyone out to dinner, and sightseeing.

Instead, we had to report to the hotel, and we had a team meeting the night before a game. Curfew was set at 11 P.M. If the game was at noon, you had from 11 until 7 A.M. to sleep. You didn't have to worry about nieces and nephews waking you up at 5:30 A.M. or your wife telling you to get up and fix breakfast or take out the trash. All you had to do was focus on the game.

After my night with the team, I came home, as I always did. I returned home at seven in the morning with the hope I could get a little more sleep. I didn't have to be at the stadium until ten. But on this particular day my mom, my brother, his wife, and his kids were staying with us, and getting any more sleep would be a challenge.

As I got ready to lay down on our bed, I noticed baby shoes with a card.

Why did my brother leave his baby's shoes on my bed? I asked myself.

I looked at the card.

"To my husband," it said.

Tina was lying on the other side of the bed.

"Congratulations," the card read. "You're a dad."

I jumped on her.

"You're pregnant again?"

She was, and I was so sure it was going to be a boy that when I went out onto the field that day, I had a bigger smile on my face than I usually had. I was so excited I said to myself, *I have to get him a touchdown.*

I had no trouble focusing on the game that day. When someone tells me I can't do something, that makes me play better. And when something happens that makes me happy, that also makes me play better.

On July 29, 2003, Tina gave birth to Cristian, the most handsome little man in the world.

The reason his name is spelled without the *h* was the result of Tina watching the soap opera *One Life to Live.* One of the characters on the show spelled his name that way, and she loved the spelling, so we copied it.

Okay, I thought. *No more kids. I got my little guy.*

AFTER MY BREAKOUT year in 2002, I was looking forward to another great year in 2003. But before the season began, tragedy struck the Packers family in a way that affected us all.

I believe in God and that everything I do is because of

Him. If I don't have a relationship with God, I can't love my wife and kids the way I'm supposed to love them. And yet, when I see bad things happen to good people, my faith is really tested. It has happened so many times.

In May 2003 I was reminded that football comes second to family when my receivers coach, Ray Sherman, lost his fourteen-year-old son, Ray Jr., who died from a self-inflicted gunshot wound. Tina and I had just arrived back in Green Bay for the off-season minicamp. The phone was ringing off the hook.

Little Ray had shot himself.

His dad was a gun owner and collector and had left an unlocked, loaded gun in his garage.

Tina and I arrived at the police station, where Ray and his wife, Yvette, were waiting. Yvette was inconsolable, and Ray was just trying to hold everything together. Tina held Yvette, and they cried. Ray and I walked around the police station. He kept asking, "Why? Why? Why did this happen?"

All I could say was "We don't know. We'll never know."

No one knew what Little Ray was doing. Was he playing with the gun? People assumed it was suicide, but if you knew Little Ray, you knew that wasn't the case. He loved life. He wasn't able to take his own life.

Ray told me he and his son were about to go to the movies to see *The Matrix*.

"Maybe Little Ray was playing, like the movies, and he pulled the trigger because he didn't check to see if there were any bullets in the gun," Ray said.

I could see a young boy doing that. What a tragedy.

. . .

WE OPENED THE 2003 season at Lambeau Field against our archrivals, the Minnesota Vikings. My whole family was in town for the game.

During the game we ran a play we called "all go," as all three of Brett's receivers headed downfield. My job was to run a seam route, to find an opening between the defenders, and as soon as I was open, Brett's job was to find me. I was running down the left sideline, and on this route Brett preferred to throw over my left, outside shoulder because my defender most likely was going to be inside on the field. I had to turn around to catch it, and when the ball came, I stopped, jumped up, and grabbed the ball, but my momentum was such that I did a complete heels over head flip.

I landed on my head, and as I lay on the ground I felt like I was paralyzed. I could see and I could hear, but I couldn't move a muscle.

"Trainers!" I could hear teammate Robert Ferguson screaming in fear. "Trainers!"

The trainers ran up to me.

"Drive, Drive!" they were yelling.

I wanted to say something, but I felt like I was asleep in a dream state.

They flipped me on my back, cut the face mask off but left my helmet on. They didn't want to risk further injury to my neck. I was carted off the field on a stretcher. The feeling in my arms and legs was beginning to return as I was being carted off.

"Give the crowd a thumbs-up to let them know you're okay," the cart driver said to me.

I did as I was told.

Tina met me as the cart rolled into the tunnel toward the locker room. She had run down from the club seats, and she had infant Cristian in her arms.

"Did I catch the ball?" I asked her.

She laughed.

"No," she said. "Coming down the ball came out."

I was in the hospital three days, and when she came and visited me, Tina was afraid for me.

"It's not worth playing this game," she said, "if you can't play with your son."

"God's not done with me," I told her. "God's going to bless us. I'm going to be okay."

I was diagnosed with a concussion, and I had a pinched nerve. The doctor said I could return in a couple of weeks.

Concussions are an unfortunate part of the game, and no matter what the NFL tries to do about it, they will always be a problem. For a long time players have been running at full speed, hitting and tackling each other, and that will never change. I applaud Commissioner Roger Goodell for trying to make the game safer with better helmets and rule changes, but as I said, no matter what they do, concussions will continue.

I didn't play in the next game against Detroit at home. During the game I walked out of the tunnel from the locker room and walked out onto the field wearing a neck brace. The crowd began to cheer. When the Packers' Robert Ferguson scored a touchdown, he high-fived everyone on the field and then ran over to me and gave me a hug.

"I'll be back," I told him. "This won't take long. I bet I'll even be back next week."

Ferguson—and everyone else—thought I was crazy.

"You can't play unless I know you can take a hit," Coach Sherman told me.

By the third day after my injury I was able to twist and turn my neck. I dressed for practice. Coach Sherman insisted that if I wanted to play against Arizona, I had to participate in the one-on-one drills. The player I had to go up against was William Henderson, who was six foot one and 252 pounds of solid muscle. William, one of the best fullbacks ever to play at Green Bay, was a battering ram. His forehead was black-and-blue from hitting people.

William and I went at it. Ten times we faced off like sumo wrestlers, only our task was to take the head off the other guy. Or rather, William's job was to take my head off.

It was a struggle to stand up to him. After every charge I had to regain my breath and compose myself. My body and neck were sore, and I left practice that day mad as a hornet that I had to face such punishment, but I didn't let anybody know. But I proved to Coach Sherman and everyone else I could play.

When I say the players feared Coach Sherman, this was but one example of it. He said I could play if I could take a hit, and he made certain I'd take a series of devastating hits. How many coaches would have tested a neck injury with such violence so soon after an injury? Not many. You could argue

143

he was looking out for me, preparing me for the game. After taking so many hits in practice, when I went out for a pass against the Arizona Cardinals, I had no fear of getting hit.

Against the Cardinals I made two catches for 12 yards. After the first catch I hit the ground and got up shaking my head.

"Are you good?" Brett asked me.

"I'm good," I said.

I was, too.

We beat the Chicago Bears the next week, and the week after that we played the Seattle Seahawks at home. I caught seven passes for 72 yards and a touchdown, but the next couple weeks we lost to Kansas City and St. Louis, and in the papers there were suggestions from the know-it-all ink-stained scribes that after signing my big contract, I wasn't the player I had been.

Who besides the writers think I'm declining? I asked myself. I was mad at everyone. It was important to prove to them I wasn't done. It was the same way I felt when my grandfather was always telling me what a loser I was going to be.

Say what you want, I will always prove you wrong.

Against the San Diego Chargers in December of that year, three months after injuring my neck, I caught eight passes for 112 yards. Then against the Oakland Raiders on Monday Night Football I played well, catching three passes for 78 yards.

The Raiders game was scheduled for December 22. The day before, Brett's father, Irvin Favre, died of a heart attack.

Kesha Peterson, a friend of mine from Cleveland, Mississippi, called me.

"Brett's father passed away," he said. "You need to find Brett."

I couldn't find Brett in his hotel room. The Packers called Doug Pederson, who was out on the golf course with Brett.

After Brett returned to our hotel from golfing, I walked down to his room and checked with his security guy to see if he was still there. When he opened the door, I could see from the expression on his face that he was hurting.

I gave him a big hug. For a long time I didn't let go.

"You know, Donald," Brett said, "I never told him I loved him."

Irvin Favre was one of those tough dads. Brett would tell stories of his toughness, how he was never the kind of guy to give him a hug or say, "I love you."

"If you don't feel like playing," I said to Brett, "we'd understand. Go home and be with your family."

Brett decided he wanted to play. He addressed the team before the game.

"I have your guys' backs, and that's why I want to play this game. I just ask that you guys have mine."

The whole room erupted. Everyone started screaming, "We've got your back, Brett. We've got your back. We love you, Brett!"

The night of the game I said to the other receivers, "Everything he throws up, we bring down regardless of how many people we have on us. Let's make history."

The first play was a corner route to tight end Wesley Walls. There was no way he should have caught it, but he did. Then on another corner route I caught a ball on the sideline over two defenders, and I was thinking, *This is ridiculous. How are we making these catches?* Javon Walker also caught one over the middle on two defenders, and before the night was out, in front of a national audience, we defeated the Oakland Raiders 41–7.

Brett completed 22 of 30 passes for 399 yards and four touchdowns. He didn't throw a single interception. His passing rating was an incredible 154.9 (perfect is 158.3). Every Packers receiver stepped up. Brett threw passes of 47 and 27 yards to Robert Ferguson, 46 and 43 yards and a touchdown to Javon Walker, and two more TDs to our tight end David Martin. They were big, big plays, all of them.

After the game, for the first time I walked into the Black Hole, Oakland's fan section, manned by rooters who seethe at opposing players. Dressed like zombies, pirates, skeletons, and the Grim Reaper, they seethe at opposing players. These crazies rose and gave Brett a standing ovation.

I was glad to be a part of that game with Brett. He showed me how a man can be with his football family.

After the game, in an emotional speech before the team in the locker room, Brett told us, "I knew that my dad would have wanted me to play. I love him so much, and I love this game. It's meant a great deal to me, to my dad, to my family, and I didn't expect this kind of performance. But I know he was watching tonight."

He said to us, "You guys are my family. I will never leave you, just like I would never leave my biological family."

Brett carried himself with such dignity and class; it was how I wanted to be. I would watch Brett to see how I should conduct myself. In the final years in Green Bay, when I wasn't getting the ball, people would ask me why I never complained.

"Because these guys are my family," I would say. "I'm not selfish. It's not just about me. It's about these guys, my family, and winning championships together."

It's what I took from Brett Favre that magical night in December 2003 on Monday Night Football.

THE PACKERS FINISHED the 2003 regular season with a 10-6 record. In the must-win season finale we killed Denver at home, 31–3, but in order to get into the playoffs we needed the Arizona Cardinals to beat Minnesota.

We were beating Denver badly toward the end of the game, but even so, Coach Sherman refused to allow the scoreboard to post the Arizona-Minnesota score. He said he wanted us concentrating on our game.

As I stood on the sideline while the defense was on the field, I could hear in the stands a murmur at first, followed by a scream and then a roar. I was looking at the defense, wondering, *What happened?* Then it dawned on me that all sixty thousand fans in the stadium were turned away from the field and toward the luxury suites where the TVs were and were getting the news that Arizona had won.

We found out later that Arizona quarterback Josh McCown threw a twenty-eight-yard touchdown pass to Nate Poole on fourth-and-twenty-five, giving the underdog Cardinals an 18–17 win. The Vikings loss gave us the NFC North division title.

Once we found out we had won, I walked over to Mike Sherman and asked him, "Can we get our hats?" The NFC North championship hats.

"Sure," he said, and while we stood on the sidelines we put them on.

We had made the playoffs. When we returned to the locker room we were able to watch Poole's catch for the final touchdown. All of us screamed and hollered.

FOOTBALL'S A FUNNY game. Going into the opening round of the 2003 playoffs against the Seattle Seahawks, we had a juggernaut on offense. Ahman Green had rushed for more than 1,800 yards on the season, and in all we ran for more than 2,500 yards and 18 touchdowns. Brett and our other quarterbacks completed 65 percent of their passes, passing for 3,300 yards and throwing 32 touchdowns.

That said, against the Seahawks the score was tied 27–27 at the end of regulation. Seattle won the coin toss at the start of overtime, and when they won it, Seattle quarterback Matt Hasselbeck told the referee, who was wearing a microphone so the national TV audience could hear him, "We want the ball, and we're going to score."

Matt should have kept his mouth shut. After 4:25 of play, Hasselbeck threw a pass that our cornerback Al Harris intercepted, and he ran it back for the game winner. It was the first time in NFL history that a playoff game was ended by a touchdown made by a defensive player.

In the locker room after the game we saw Matt's comment on ESPN. Our guys said, "I can't believe he has an ego like that."

"He should have kept his mouth shut" was my response.

IN THE NEXT round we faced the Philadelphia Eagles, led by quarterback Donovan McNabb. If we won, we were sure we'd get to the Super Bowl because the Carolina Panthers were next, and we had their number. With our combustible offense, led by Brett, we didn't see how we could lose.

We led 14–7 at the half, and we should have had another touchdown when the Eagles stopped Ahman at their one on fourth down. We still led, now 17–14, with only 1:12 left in the game. The Eagles had a fourth and 26.

"We're going to the NFC championship, baby," I told Brett. "No, we're going to the Super Bowl."

"Yes," Brett yelled. "This game is *over.*"

When we got the ball back we were going to take a knee and run out the clock.

I watched calmly as McNabb dropped back to pass. He threw a long pass downfield. The ball floated in the air an interminable amount of time. Eagles receiver Freddie Mitchell made the catch.

It can't possibly be a first down, I said to myself.

The referee marked the ball. They checked the chains. First down, Eagles. The pass had gone for 28 yards.

"You . . . have . . . got . . . to . . . be . . . kidding," I said.

"Wow," said Brett.

The Eagles' David Akers kicked a thirty-seven-yard field goal to tie it in regulation play, and they went on to win it in overtime on another Akers field goal as the mob in Philadelphia went wild. All we could do was trudge back to our locker room with our tail between our legs. It was devastating. It was my best chance to go to the Super Bowl. It was a sad ending to a beautiful season.

For any NFL player the greatest milestone is to make it to the Super Bowl. We all dream of making it there one day. We always question ourselves, *Will that day ever come?* That is because most athletes who play in the NFL never make it there. And it was where I wanted to be. Did I think it would ever happen? You could wish and hope, but you never really did know.

Most fans don't understand just how difficult it is to reach the Super Bowl. People think that just because their team is talented, it's going to get there. That's what I thought when I first came to Green Bay in 1999. The Packers had been in back-to-back Super Bowls in 1997 and 1998, and my first thoughts were, *These guys just came back from two Super Bowls. We're going to be going back my rookie year. It's going to be awesome.*

And I didn't make it to the Super Bowl for twelve years.

WHEN THE 2004 season began I saw that I would have to prove myself all over again. Maybe it was because after gaining 1,064 yards in 2002, I followed that with a year in which I only gained 621 yards in receptions. Maybe my neck injury had something to do with that. All I knew was that Javon Walker was projected to start over me in 2004, even though

Right: Posing for a photo before my high school prom. As you can see, I've always been a sharp dresser! *(Donald Driver Foundation)*

Bottom left: Me and my cousin Johnny White, before an Easter Sunday church service. Faith played a major role in my upbringing and continues to be a very important part of my life. *(Donald Driver Foundation)*

Bottom right: Me (left), sharing some food in my grandma's kitchen with Moses and my cousin "Bug." *(Donald Driver Foundation)*

Above: In college, I was a two-sport athlete: a wide receiver for the football team and a high jumper in track and field. I even contemplated quitting football in 2000 to try out for the Sydney Olympics. *(Herald/ASU)*

Below: Standing with my grandparents George and Betty Lofton as they proudly display my diploma from Alcorn State. My grandfather never saw me play a football game. Of all my achievements, this was the one he was most proud of. *(Donald Driver Foundation)*

After watching 212 players get picked before me in the 1999 NFL draft, I finally received a phone call from the Green Bay General Manager Ron Wolf and learned I would become a Packer. *(Donald Driver Foundation)*

During my first season in 1999 I was assigned the number 13. I always thought it was to signify my rank among receivers on the depth chart. (There were thirteen receivers on the roster during training camp.) *(Jim Biever)*

I spent much of my first year with the Packers on special teams, but I finally got the chance to play receiver during a game late in the 1999 season. I scored a touchdown on my very first catch. *(Rick Wood/Milwaukee Journal Sentinel)*

Left: In 2003, I was carted off the field wearing a neck brace after suffering this hard hit on a drive against Minnesota. *(Jim Biever)*

Below: Brett Favre and me taking in the action from the sidelines during a game against the Chiefs in 2007. Brett and I became great friends, but the 2007 season was the last time the two of us would play together, as he was traded to the New York Jets the following off-season. *(Jim Biever)*

During our summer training camp, young Packers fans line up outside our practice facilities with their bikes. Before practices, we would ride across the street to Lambeau Field while the kids walked, jogged, or in this case, Rollerbladed alongside. I think I loved it as much as the kids! *(Jim Biever)*

Sharing a special moment with the fans after a home game in 2007. One of the main reasons I never played for another team was the amount of love the fans showed me throughout my career. They deserved to see me retire having worn only the green and gold. *(Mary Jo Walicki/*Milwaukee Journal Sentinel)

Racing past a defender on my way to scoring a 90-yard touchdown in the 2008 NFC Championship Game. The play still stands as the longest play from scrimmage In Packers playoff history. *(Jim Biever)*

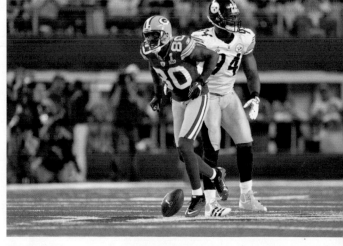

Celebrating after making a first down reception in the 2011 Super Bowl. *(Jim Biever)*

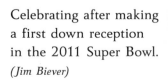

Nothing felt sweeter than lifting the Lombardi Trophy after we defeated the Pittsburgh Steelers in Super Bowl XLV, 31–25. This moment is what I spent my whole career working for . . . and it was 100 percent worth it! *(AP Images)*

Setting the Packers franchise all-time record for receiving yards against Carolina in 2011. *(Streeter Lecka/Getty Images)*

Here I am having some fun with a fan while performing the "Lambeau Leap" in 2013. The Lambeau Leap is a Packers' tradition, performed after a player scores a touchdown. *(AP Images)*

Initially I didn't want to have children because of the struggles I went through when I was young, but today, Betina and I are the proud parents of three beautiful children (clockwise from top: Charity, Cristian, and Christina). It was the best decision I ever made! *(Accent Photography by Kim)*

In 2012, I joined the cast of ABC's *Dancing with the Stars*. My partner, Peta Murgatroyd, and I would go on to win the competition along with the coveted Mirror Ball trophy. *(Adam Taylor/© American Broadcasting Companies, Inc.)*

Bringing kids into the huddle at one of my football camps. I'm blessed to be able to hold these free of charge and around the country every year. *(Donald Driver Foundation)*

Top: Kicking a soccer ball to a group of kids on a charity trip to Africa in 2009. Even though a lot of these kids lived in some of the worst poverty you can imagine, they still had huge smiles on their faces. *(Donald Driver Foundation)*

Center: Scoring a run against my Packer teammates in the 2012 Donald Driver Softball Game, one of my favorite days of the year. The annual game, which pits members of the Packers' offense vs. the defense, has helped raise over $1 million for the Donald Driver Foundation and other local charities. *(Donald Driver Foundation)*

Bottom: Me and Betina at the White House Correspondents' Dinner. *(Jennifer Wishon/CBN News)*

he was having problems with his eyesight and was having trouble holding on to the ball. Robert Ferguson was supposed to be the other starter at wide receiver. In the preseason I beat out Robert and never looked back.

Our first game was against the Carolina Panthers, and I started along with Javon. That year we made a dynamic duo. He caught passes for 1,382 yards and 12 touchdowns, and I caught 84 balls for 1,208 yards. We again finished with a fine 10-6 record, but we lost to Minnesota badly in the first round of the playoffs. Coach Mike Sherman's reign as head coach was coming to an end.

One of the problems was that Ron Wolf quit as general manager in 2003. I was devastated. I never thought he'd leave. I figured he'd be my general manager until the day I retired. But Ron said he wanted to retire so he could go and do other things. He had said to me, "I'm going to get you that big contract." He left before I got it, but I know he was the one pushing for it. It felt so good when the guy who believes in you gets you the deal.

After Ron retired, Mike badly wanted the job of general manager as well as the head coaching job. It's a mistake a number of successful head coaches have made, because it's extremely difficult to fill both shoes. As general manager you have to tell your players why they don't deserve the money they are asking for, and then as coach you have to tell them how terrific they are. You can't negotiate a guy's contract, beat his brains in, and then expect him to be receptive when you're trying to teach him something about football. By the end of the 2004 season the Packers' top brass stripped Mike of his GM duties. He was replaced as GM by Ted Thompson, who was hired away from the Seattle Seahawks.

I suspect Thompson and Sherman didn't get along. When someone comes in and takes your job, you're never happy.

The 2005 season was a disaster. We finished the season 4-12, losing seven of our first eight games and dooming Mike Sherman's reign as head coach of the Packers.

"The coaches don't play the game. The players play the game," I've always said, but sometimes the scheme, the play-calling, doesn't work in your favor for sixteen games. But unless the team doesn't have the tools to win, you shouldn't lose twelve of those games, and we certainly had the weapons to win. We just didn't play to our potential, and though the fault lies with both the coach and the players, we always say, "The head coach will be gone before the players will be gone." That's how it is. You can't play in the NFL without players. You can always get another coach.

I don't remember games from 2005. I don't even remember plays. I did what I could to block it all out. It was so bad. I do remember that in our first game against Detroit, Javon Walker injured his right knee and was lost for the season. Robert Ferguson and Ahman Green also were injured and that made winning a lot harder.

We defeated Seattle in the final game, and I was figuring that Mike's job was safe. Because of the many injuries we had that season I thought to myself, *No way Mike Sherman should lose his job.*

The Monday after we beat the Seahawks to end the season, I walked into Lambeau to collect my things and clear out my locker. We had a team meeting scheduled for 10:15 A.M., and I figured that meant Mike was still our coach. They then pushed the meeting back to 10:35, and at that point I figured he was toast.

After we gathered for the meeting our new general manager, Ted Thompson, walked in and announced, "We have just let Mike Sherman go."

Frank Novak, one of Mike's assistants and a close confidant, stood up.

"When that man walks through that door," he said, "I want everybody to get up out of your seat and give this man what he deserves."

Novak was right. Mike Sherman deserved everyone's respect. We had won a lot of games under his leadership. We just didn't make it to the Super Bowl.

When Mike walked in, everyone rose and clapped for him. The emotion was genuine. We respected him greatly. He had helped make me the player I became.

The next day Tina, my two kids, and I were in the airport for our flight home when I spotted Mike. He was putting his teenage daughter on a plane to send her back to college. After he hugged his daughter, he hugged me.

"I'm so proud of you," he said to me. "When I walked in the building I didn't even know who you were."

His eyes were watery. He was terribly hurt by being let go. I could see it written all over his face.

CHAPTER 9

MY
GLORY
YEARS

WHEN MIKE MCCARTHY became the Packers' head coach in 2006, he wasn't a total stranger. Mike had been the quarterback coach for the Packers in 1999, and I can remember him standing with Brett and Doug Pederson joking and laughing. He wasn't the martinet that Mike Sherman was. He was more like an older brother who came to you with advice. He was always coaching, working with guys, though Brett was a veteran who didn't need much help.

Mike McCarthy had left the Packers the year Ray Rhodes was fired, and he went to New Orleans as their offensive coordinator. A friend of mine, Aaron Brooks, was very upset when he was traded to New Orleans just after Mike signed to be their coach, and I told Aaron, "Mike is a great guy. He's going to take care of you over there."

I would watch the Saints on TV, and I could see Mike on the sidelines talking with and listening to his players. That was the thing about Mike. He would ask what you were thinking, and he would listen to his players, whether you were a rookie or a veteran. I will always be grateful to Mike for coming in and allowing me to continue as a primary receiver. I was thirty years old, and he could have buried me for a younger man. It was Mike McCarthy who allowed me to forge my legacy.

After coaching in New Orleans Mike was hired for the

same offensive coordinator job with the San Francisco 49ers. His specialty was developing quarterbacks and offenses. He brought with him to Green Bay the famed West Coast offense, one that emphasized passing over the running game. Under McCarthy, Brett Favre developed into the finest quarterback in the NFL.

Brett was a wonderful teammate. He was the funniest guy I ever played with. He kept things lively. He loved putting a whoopee cushion under the cushion of your chair. He put live rats in teammates' lockers. He kept guys laughing all the time.

One year, on his birthday in October, Brett was running around the locker room chasing teammates and throwing handfuls of cake. I was sitting on the training table minding my own business, laughing at what they were doing, when Brett came running over and jammed a piece of gooey cake into my face.

I was mad. It was good cake he was wasting.

"What are you thinking?" I yelled at him. "We have to go to practice."

Not wanting to be late, I ran out with cake and frosting all over my face.

The coaches sent me back to clean up.

I got even. Before practice soon afterward, I swiped Brett's helmet from his locker, and I coated it with Zostrix, an arthritis pain medication. When you put it on your skin and you get sweaty, it burns like fire ants. I put his helmet back in his locker.

I warned the trainers not to say anything.

"Not one word," I told them.

After we ran some drills, Brett started to heat up.

"What's wrong, Brett?" I asked him.

"I feel like I have a fever," he said.

"Yeah, it's hot out here today," I said.

The trainers, afraid he'd burn up, spilled the beans. His forehead was smoking red. After that Brett never messed with me again. He said he'd get even, but he never did.

Brett and I became veterans together. Before 2006 Brett had sat on the plane rides next to backup quarterback Doug Pederson. After Doug retired after the 2005 season, Brett sat in his usual seat. Pointing to the seat next to his, he said to me, "Drive, sit here." I did as I was told.

I had been sitting with Rob Davis, our long snapper.

"Oh sure, you're going to leave me," Rob said to me.

Brett and I sat together until he left the Packers. Brett wasn't a card player. He liked to do crossword puzzles. I read books. Sometimes he'd take out his laptop and watch game video. Often we'd talk football. He'd discuss our plays and what he expected when he called a particular play.

"If this defender jumps," he would say, "I'm throwing to you."

Working with Brett, one of the greatest ever to play the game, was a career highlight. Being close to him as a friend made playing with him more special.

My wife, Tina, is from Mississippi, and Brett and his wife, Deanna, are, too. We would visit them in Hattiesburg.

The first time we visited him, he asked me to go hunting with him.

"I don't know about that," I said. "You don't see black people hunting."

He tried to convince me to go by telling me how much fun it was to walk around the hundreds of acres he lives on, climb a tree, and wait for a deer to come by.

"The thing is, Brett," I told him, "I don't like being up in trees, sitting there all day, trying to shoot something that probably won't come by anyway."

Brett thought that perhaps I'd enjoy a run through his woods.

"You go out there walking through the trees," he said, "and you'll send the deer toward me."

I thought he was out of his mind.

"Look at me," I said. "Do you see what color I am? I'm blacker than the deer. If I run through these woods, someone will take a shot at me because they think I'm a deer. I'm going to be dead, and it's going to be your fault."

Brett spent the afternoon driving me around his property.

We might not have had hunting in common, but we certainly had winning in common. We were on the field together for eighty-eight Packers victories. When I first arrived in Green Bay, Brett told me I was a great athlete and that I would be a fine pro player. Once I became a regular, he would continually work with me on our communication.

"Donald, if I peek at you," he'd say in the huddle, "I'm coming to you. If I give you a wink or if I look at you and turn my head, I'm coming at you."

After a while people would wonder, *How in the heck did Donald know what Brett was going to do?*

I read his energy. I also had to learn to keep a sharp eye out on him. My second year in the league in a game against Carolina, Brett was running to his right, and I was all the way to the left in the corner of the end zone, when I knew I could get open by running to the middle of the field. Brett drilled a throw straight down the field that hit me for a touchdown.

Look at this guy, I marveled. *How does he do it?*

I learned always to keep my eyes on him. He could be on the run, about to fall, and then he'd toss you a bullet for a completion. He would constantly advise, "Stay with me. Never take your eyes off me."

Another piece of advice: "Don't ever stop running." And I wouldn't. I knew if I kept running, eventually the man would find me.

THE YEAR 2006 could well have been a disaster, but it ended on a high note. We began the season 1-4. After a bye week, we traveled to Miami to play the Dolphins.

One play may have turned around our season. With the score tied 10–10 in the third quarter, Brett threw the ball to me in the end zone on a corner route between two defenders for a thirty-four-yard touchdown. I caught the ball with one hand, and after I was tackled the referees were saying the ball had hit the ground and the pass was incomplete.

I got up from the play screaming bloody murder.

I ran to Coach McCarthy.

"Did you catch it?" he wanted to know. If you made a challenge and weren't upheld, it cost the team a valued time-out.

"Throw the flag!" I screamed. "I caught it. Look at my

arm. It's the same color as that ball. They saw my arm hit the ground—not the ball."

The replay showed I did catch the ball, and when the referee signaled a touchdown Brett ran over to me, scooped me up, and started running around the field as I dangled upside down in his arms. I felt ridiculous.

"Put me down," I told him.

The touchdown helped us beat the Dolphins 34–24 and stop our losing streak.

It was a special game for me. I had a game-high ten catches for 93 yards, and I became only the seventh player in Packers history to gain 5,000 receiving yards.

The next week we were home at Lambeau Field against the Arizona Cardinals when on a naked bootleg Brett ran into the end zone for a touchdown.

After he scored, I pointed to the stands and told him, "Go."

He did as he was told. He jumped among the delirious Packers fans. It was Brett's first and only time he did the Lambeau Leap during his long career. That's when I realized he and I had built a special bond. No two teammates could be closer.

We won our last four games of the 2006 season to finish the year a respectable 8–8. With those four wins, we knew we were building toward something special in 2007.

When minicamp rolled around the critics predicted we'd continue being a .500 team, but when Brett looked around and saw our lineup, he commented to me that he thought this was the most talented team he'd ever been on.

Playing with Brett his final year in Green Bay was special

and memorable. It was his seventeenth year in the league, and in week two, against the New York Giants, he got his 149th win, surpassing John Elway as the winningest quarterback in NFL history. In week four, against Minnesota in the Metrodome, Brett threw a touchdown to Greg Jennings, the 421st touchdown of his career, to break the all-time NFL record of 420, set by Dan Marino.

There was a three-week span in the middle of the season when he threw for 1,042 yards. At thirty-eight years of age he had a passer rating of 100 or more in ten games. Brett was superb all year long.

In 2007 we had one of the best—though youngest—receiving corps in the NFL. We had second-year wide-out Greg Jennings, myself, veteran Koren Robinson, and two rookies: James Jones and Ruvell Martin. We had a great bond.

I became the Packers' slot receiver, whose job it is to find the spaces between defenders in the middle of the field. After you catch the ball you are subject to violent hits to the head, neck, and chest from linebackers and safeties who are flying at you from all directions.

When you play the slot, you have to concern yourself with a lot more detail than if you're a flanker or a split end. You have to read what the linebackers, corners, and safeties are doing. The flanker and split ends are the speed guys, the ones who run down the field and clear everything out. The slot is Mr. Reliable, the guy who keeps a drive going. I had to know how to maneuver in the middle of the field, to run the right route and also sometimes to make a key block. I had to block linebackers, many of whom were fifty pounds heavier than I was.

You have to be tough to play the slot. You have to be willing to work the middle of the field knowing you're going to get your head knocked off. It's a position not every receiver is willing to play—Javon Walker and Corey Bradford didn't want any part of it—because you're likely to be clobbered by a hulking linebacker or even a monstrous defensive lineman like Warren Sapp, who once tackled me and tried to crush me. Fortunately I saw him coming. I tried to make a move, but Sapp grabbed me, brought me down, and put all of his three hundred pounds on top of me.

"Man, get your sweaty butt off of me!" I yelled at him.

Sapp just laughed and growled, "Driiivvve."

WE HAD BEGUN the season with a 7-1 record in 2007 when we played the Minnesota Vikings at home on November 11. In that game Coach McCarthy unveiled his "Big Five" package, with five offensive linemen, all five of us receivers, and Brett.

Coach McCarthy came to us with the reputation of being an expert in the West Coast offense. The high-powered, passing-oriented philosophy has a long and glorious history. It was invented by Sid Gilman, coach of the San Diego Chargers, in the 1960s; his assistant, Al Davis, continued to use it to terrorize the league after he took over the Oakland Raiders. Davis was the one who invented the slot formation, with two fast receivers on one side flooding an area.

Don Coryell employed the offense when he was at San Diego State University, and one of his assistants there, John Madden, went to the Oakland Raiders and made it famous.

Another Al Davis assistant, Bill Walsh of Stanford, improved it even more. Walsh had a handful of disciples including coach Paul Hackett, and when Hackett and McCarthy were together as coaches of the Kansas City Chiefs, McCarthy learned it from Hackett.

Coach McCarthy knew everyone's strengths and weaknesses. He would put you in the right position to make plays to win games. McCarthy was amazing.

OUR RECORD IN 2007 was 13-3, and yet for some reason the game I remember most vividly was a terrible loss we suffered at the hands of the Chicago Bears in late December. The game was played at Soldier Field and it was sixteen degrees out. With the windchill, it felt like minus thirteen. It was brutally cold.

We were already in the playoffs, knew we had a first-round bye, and figured the game didn't mean anything to us. I decided I would have as much fun as possible playing the game, but the freezing weather made that almost impossible.

The wind of Lake Michigan was blowing hard, and my toes were numb. I put my foot in the heater on the sidelines, and my shoestrings caught on fire. I was so numb I didn't feel the flames.

Going back into the game, all I could think was, *What am I doing out here? They should cancel this game.*

During halftime I was happy to be in the locker room out of the cold. When it was time to start the second half, some of us stayed inside until the very last moment. For the kickoff I ran straight from the locker room onto the field. Mike McCarthy was furious.

What the crap is going on? he was wondering.

Brett threw two interceptions, we had two punts blocked, and we lost the game 35–7. Afterward in the locker room, Coach McCarthy screamed himself hoarse for our coming out of the locker room late and for losing so badly.

We were thinking, *Hey, Mike, we're already in the playoffs. It doesn't matter,* but our attitude was very wrong. It mattered because it was a game against our rival, Chicago, and because no matter who we were playing, we should always play hard for the fans.

The next week we returned home to Lambeau Field and beat the Detroit Lions 34–14. Brett threw two touchdown passes and left the game at the start of the second quarter. It was our seventeenth consecutive home win against Detroit. We were ready for the playoffs.

ON JANUARY 12, 2008, we hosted our former coach, Mike Holmgren, and the Seattle Seahawks in an afternoon game that was played in a near blizzard. Fat snowflakes fell steadily. It wasn't all that cold, about thirty-one degrees, which in Green Bay is like a spring day, and there was no wind. Lambeau Field looked like one of those snow globes. You couldn't see the lines on the field. Everything in front of you was—white.

Our star rookie running back, Ryan Grant, fumbled twice, helping to give the Seahawks a 14–0 lead. But Ryan redeemed himself and then some, rushing for 201 yards and three touchdowns. Greg Jennings also had a great game, catching balls for 71 yards and two touchdowns.

We needed just one more win against the New York Giants at home, and we'd be in the Super Bowl playing the 18-0 New England Patriots, with quarterback Tom Brady and his star receiver, Randy Moss.

The game against the Giants was played at 6:30 P.M. Darkness was falling, and so were the temperatures. It was even colder than it had been in Chicago on that horrible day. It was minus one degree at kickoff, with temperatures dropping even further as the game went on. It was the second-coldest game in NFL history, after the legendary Ice Bowl game between the Cowboys and the Packers in 1967.

The game should have been canceled. It was inhumane to make us play under such conditions. At the same time we were all very aware of the advantage we had playing in such cold weather. We knew most of the visiting teams weren't used to it.

In the 1990s and 2000s the Packers had an advantage over any team coming from the South. Miami or Tampa Bay played most of their games in warmer weather, so when they came to Lambeau Field and had to face twelve degrees with a windchill of minus twenty-one, they weren't used to it. Tampa Bay *never* won in Green Bay. Their players would wear long-sleeve shirts or tights. We didn't need that. It was more of a mind game than anything. We felt we could play in it. The other team felt they couldn't. And they just couldn't beat us, even when they might have had a better team.

It was the same way with teams that played in domed stadiums, among them the Minnesota Vikings, Detroit Lions, and New Orleans Saints, who played their eight home games inside. During the season those teams might have two games where they have to play in cold weather, and that was in Green Bay and Chicago. We had an advantage over those guys as well. Detroit, for one, *never* beat us at home. One time when they were 0-15, they had a chance to beat us. They were ahead, and I caught a seven-yard touchdown pass to win the game and drop them to 0-16. I cherished that for a long time.

Whoever came to Green Bay in November and December, it was a guarantee we were going to win. They couldn't stop us, because they weren't used to the cold.

The only team in our division that wasn't a dome team was the Chicago Bears, and we knew that whenever we played the Bears it would be a battle, in large part because the Bears also practiced in cold weather.

The Giants played outdoors, but it usually wasn't as cold in New York as it was in Green Bay. Going into the game, we still felt we held the advantage because of the weather.

Red Batty, our equipment manager, cut seams in the sides of our jerseys and added a pouch of fur inside the fronts. For the pregame we kept our hands in there, and it felt very good. If you can feel your hands, the rest doesn't matter. We all had our hands in that pouch in the huddle.

One of the highlights of the game was a ninety-yard touchdown pass Brett threw to me. Corey Webster, the Giants cornerback, tried to jam me at the line, but I was able to get past him, and after Brett found me with the pass twenty yards downfield, I outran the three Giants chasing me. I scored, and I performed the Lambeau Leap, but it was so cold I was gasping for breath as I landed in the stands.

It was the longest pass in Packers playoff history, and I had to take a couple of plays off during the next drive just to catch my breath.

We led at halftime 10–6, and after the Giants scored, Brett threw a touchdown to tight end Donald Lee to put us back in front. The Giants took the lead again with a touchdown run. Our kicker, Mason Crosby, tied the game with a thirty-seven-yard field goal. The game ended in regulation tied 20–20.

In overtime Brett threw an interception that everyone remembers to this day. It was the last pass of his long and illustrious Packers career. The ball he threw was directed toward me.

I ran a shake route to the post, turned, and headed to the corner. I beat Corey Webster, gave him a post move, and ran underneath him. I looked back at Brett, and he let fire, and I knew, *If I catch this ball, I've got a touchdown, and we're going to the Super Bowl.*

Brett didn't put his usual zing on the ball. He didn't step into the throw. The ball floated. As it left Brett's hand, I was saying to myself, *Nooooooo,* and as I stood there waiting for the ball to reach me, I was helpless to do anything when Webster, who was positioned on my right hip, caught the ball in front of me. I tried to strip the ball so he'd drop it, but he balled up around the football and fell to the ground.

On the sidelines Greg Jennings came over and tried to put a positive spin on what was happening.

"We're going to the Super Bowl, Drive," he said. "We're going."

I was less sure. The Giants had missed two field goals in regulation that would have won it for them.

"God gave us two chances," I said to Greg. "I doubt if He's going to give us a third."

And He didn't.

Giants field goal kicker Lawrence Tynes drilled a forty-seven-yarder through the uprights, a kick frozen in time. I can still see that ball flying through the air straight and true.

My head dropped. I sat on the Packers bench for a long time after the game had ended. Jennings had to come over and drag me inside. In the locker room I sat there stunned.

You've got to be kidding me, I kept saying to myself.

We had planned for our trip to Arizona for the Super Bowl. It was arranged that at the end of this game we were going to stand out in the middle of the field with the NFC Championship trophy and celebrate with our frozen, frostbitten fans.

Our planning was for nothing, I thought. I could not believe that we had lost. *How did we lose this game?* I sat in front of my locker and cried. After years and years this was my opportunity to go to the Super Bowl. I was counting on it. And we had let it slip away. The worst part: Brett and I once again didn't get to go to the Super Bowl together, and now we never would.

CHAPTER 10

BRETT RETIRES— THEN DOESN'T

My CAREER IN football has allowed me to meet some very incredible people throughout the years. One was Barack Obama, whom I met when he was a U.S. senator from Illinois, campaigning in Dallas for the presidency in 2008. When nice guy Reggie Love was trying out with the Packers as a receiver in 2006, he told me he was going to write to Senator Obama to ask him for a job.

"He could be the first black president," Reggie said to me.

"Yeah, right, Reggie," I said. "A black president. That will *never* happen."

Well, Reggie got a job all right. He became Obama's personal assistant during the presidential campaign. He and Obama played basketball nearly every day, always on the same side, and it was his job to make sure he met all of Obama's needs.

In early 2008, I walked into a room in the American Airlines Center arena in Dallas, where Obama was campaigning, and I saw Reggie.

"Drive," he said, and we hugged. I couldn't believe he was working with Obama.

"I told you I'd do this," he said.

Senator Obama joined us. It was Reggie's job as his right-hand man to know everybody in the room and point them out and brief Obama.

When Obama came to me, the first thing he said was "I don't like you."

Why not? was what I was thinking. I hadn't put it together.

"Because, Donald," he said, "I'm a Chicago Bears fan. I haven't liked you for years. In fact, I can't stand you. Every time I thought the Bears were going to pull it out, you'd break our backs with a touchdown."

We laughed about it, and he even mentioned me and Cowboy great Emmitt Smith, who was also there, in his speech.

"We're going to partner with Emmitt Smith and Donald Driver," he said, and the crowd went wild. Tina was so excited she punched me in the leg. I felt like someone special.

Two years later, before we played the Washington Redskins, then–San Francisco 49ers wide receiver Brett Swain and one of his friends arranged for Aaron Rodgers, our receivers coach Jimmy Robinson, and the Packers receiving corps to be invited to the White House for a special tour.

We walked the gardens and we saw the library, and in the middle of the tour President Obama stopped by.

"I was hoping there were a bunch of Bears players," he said, "but when I found out you were Packers, I almost walked away." He said the only reason he didn't keep walking is that he knew one of the Packers.

"How are you, Donald?" he asked.

He had remembered Tina and me from Dallas, and we both got hugs. The rest of the group was stunned.

President Obama greeted everyone else and was charming. He asked if I was still playing. I told him I was.

"How old are you? Fifty?" he asked.

"Close to it," I said, grinning.

When he left I had to explain to everyone how I knew the president.

I was in Dallas in March 2008 when Brett Favre announced at a press conference he was retiring. It was a surprise but I wasn't shocked because he had played a long time and had done everything a player could possibly do. He had played in 273 games in a row, a record that will never be broken. He hadn't missed a start since 1992.

They're going to retire his jersey, I thought. *He's going to the Hall of Fame. What else does he have to prove?*

Nothing.

Brett normally isn't an emotional guy, and I felt for him as I watched him weep. As I watched him I thought, *Football is all the man knows. What's he going to do?*

When he was home in Mississippi, he was in his barn all day or sitting on his tractor or cutting something down or burning something or shooting at something.

What's he going to do without football? I wondered. He wasn't going to be a broadcaster or go back to school or start some business.

I had some doubts about his retiring when around the Fourth of July Brett announced he had changed his mind, that he wanted to play another season for the Packers.

There was a problem, though—the Packers announced that they had committed to Brett's backup, Aaron Rodgers. The Packers didn't want Brett back!

Brett asked for his outright release. The Packers refused. When training camp began in the summer of 2008, we came to camp and left Brett sitting at home in Hattiesburg. Packers fans were split. About half wanted him back as our quarterback; the other half wanted Aaron, a young, talented kid.

Reporters kept asking me what I thought about the situation. I knew I had to be careful. I was close friends with Brett, but I didn't want to seem disloyal to the organization and didn't want to burn bridges.

"I want to play football" was my middle-of-the-road answer. "That's what I do."

I was very much going to miss Brett. I never took him for granted. But at the end of the day it didn't matter who was throwing to me. I had learned my lesson from a comment I had made three years earlier when I was asked whether Brett was going to retire.

Stupidly I had said, "He might."

Mike Sherman was ticked off at me for saying that and read me the riot act.

This time I was staying out of it.

IN THE END the Packers traded Brett to the New York Jets, where he played for a year. The next year he came out of retirement for a second time and joined the hated Minnesota Vikings for a season.

The first time we played the Vikings when Brett was with them I looked across the field, and there he was, wearing his number 4 in a Vikings uniform.

Is that really my guy over there in that purple? I wondered.

Brett was masterful in the game, throwing three touchdowns and beating us. After the game we gave each other a big hug.

"You don't look good in purple," I told him.

He laughed.

"Keep doing what you're doing," he said.

Knowing what I know and how it all ended between Brett and the Packers, I don't know what either side really could have done. Brett wanted to play in Green Bay. The Packers wanted to get younger and give Aaron Rodgers the opportunity to grow and develop. He could not have done that if Brett had continued as a Packer. Brett and the Packers had a sixteen-year marriage, and the Packers divorced him.

His leaving and playing for New York and Minnesota won't tarnish his legacy in Green Bay. One day Brett's number will be retired here, and he will receive long and loud applause. He was cheered when he came back as a Viking! He came through the tunnel, and the crowd cheered him.

There is still bitterness on Brett's part, but sooner or later the bitterness will fade. It's just a question of when. Maybe Ted Thompson has to be gone or maybe Coach McCarthy or maybe Aaron. I don't know. But I do know Brett Favre's number will be retired by the Packers. No other Packer will ever wear jersey 4.

Brett built the franchise after years of mediocrity. He will always be a legend in Green Bay.

• • •

BRETT'S ANNOUNCED RETIREMENT—or so we all thought—meant that Aaron Rodgers, the Packers' first-round draft pick from 2005, would be our starting quarterback for the 2008 season.

Aaron attended a press conference for a Fan Fest event at Lambeau.

"I know I have the support of the team because I have received so many supportive text messages from the players," Aaron said.

One of those messages came from me.

In my first text I said to him, "Don't worry about what people say. We have your back. I love you, and I will always love you."

I also told Aaron I needed him.

"I need you too," he texted me back.

Sometimes players show support like that because they want to lead and it's the right thing to do. I did it because I genuinely believed in the guy and wanted him to know it.

A lot of people wondered whether I'd take to Aaron because I had been so close to Brett. Even Aaron had that concern. When Aaron joined the team he was a very confident twenty-one-year-old who felt he should have been the first player taken above all others in the 2005 draft. He came on like *Hey, I'm Aaron Rodgers. I'm supposed to be the first pick of the draft. I shouldn't have been here. But I'm here.*

We were lucky enough get him as the twenty-fourth pick.

Brett and Aaron aren't the same person. They play different. Brett plays the game hard-nosed, and you don't find many guys like that. Brett played in 255 Green Bay Packers games, the most of any Packer in history, fifty more than me, who is second. Guys like that are rare. Brett is the true Iron Man of the National Football League.

Brett was a renegade who wasn't afraid to take chances. When I played with him, plenty of times I would have three defenders covering me, and he'd throw it to me anyway because he had trust in me that I'd make the catch. His attitude was *The guy can make plays, and I'm going to get him the ball.* Of course, every once in a while the pass would be intercepted, but that was just the way Brett played.

What Aaron Rodgers brings to the table is his unwillingness to take wild chances. He takes exactly what the defense gives him. He's going to follow orders. If I had three guys on me, Aaron never would throw me the ball. It wasn't that Aaron didn't trust me. It was more his conservative nature. When Brett was quarterback, Aaron would say to me, "I don't like you, but I'm pulling for you today." At the same time during home games when they announced the lineups, Aaron and I would give each other a hug. When Aaron became the starting quarterback we dropped the "I don't like you" part of the ritual.

"I love you," I would say.

"I love you, too," he'd say back. "Let's go do what we do."

As a result the transition from Brett to Aaron was easy.

I saw the kid grow, and he became something special.

AFTER THE 2007 football season, Tina and I were invited to visit Africa by World Vision, a charity organization that helps people around the world with clothing, food, water wells, and other needs. I've always had a curiosity about Africa, and in May 2008, Green Bay defensive lineman Aaron Kampman and his wife, Linde; Troy Murphy, one of the pastors of Community Church in Green Bay, and his wife; and Tina and I traveled to Kenya on a fact-finding mission to determine the needs of its people.

We landed in Nairobi and prepared for a six-hour car ride to Mutombo. We were told the ride would be bumpy, that the last four hours would be over dirt roads. I didn't know what to expect. All I knew about Africa was safaris.

We were riding in the middle car of a three-truck caravan. All the luggage was in the third car. After two hours of driving, the paved roads gave way to dirt. We stopped at one of the last stores, bought some snacks, and hit the road because we were told to get to our destination before nightfall.

The driver really pushed, not allowing us to stop. My driver was talking by phone intensely to the driver in the lead car, and I had to know why. It turned out that parts of Kenya are dangerous to visitors.

We had been told to put all our money, passports, and IDs in money belts. The reason, we found out, is that there were guards at checkpoints who could stop you and, if they felt like it, confiscate your bags. We were told that in most of Kenya, credit cards weren't accepted. Cash only.

As we passed one town with farmland dotted by little huts, little kids were running up to us screaming. We waved back.

The police stopped us, looked us over, and sent us through. We continued driving until we came upon uniformed guards, armed to the teeth with AK-47s, who stopped us, looked us over, and again sent us on our way. We still had our luggage, I was glad to say.

It started to get dark just as we drove through a little neighborhood.

"We have to keep going," said the driver.

After another hour he pulled up to an old, metal-gated fence that surrounded a giant brick wall.

"We're staying here," he said.

"Go get drinks and dinner," we were told. "Not to worry."

And so I didn't.

Inside the compound chickens were running around, and cats were everywhere. Tina doesn't like cats, and so she was jumpy, looking everywhere for them.

They served chicken with sauce and rice in a bowl. For dessert we had some kind of melon I had never seen before. I was still hungry.

I was tired from the long drive. I asked to be taken to my hut because I knew I had some snacks in my bag. By now it was pitch-dark. There were no lights. A guide with a flashlight led Tina and me to our room, which was pitch-black inside.

I hit the light switch. I heard a crack and a buzz and a ding as one little lightbulb went on. Then we heard the sounds of *things* scurrying about.

I have no idea what they were. I never saw them.

"Make sure you zip up your bags after you get something from them," said our guide. "You don't want anything to crawl into your bags."

The light on, I looked around the mud hut. Besides the bed there wasn't one single stick of furniture. I asked if there was a chair or bench we could put our bags on.

"We don't have anything," said the guide.

We went back outside and spent an hour or so talking with the other members of the group. Finally our eyes got heavy, and we returned to our room.

Tina wanted to take a bath. I turned on the water for her. Out came little drips of water. I held a flashlight to make sure no creatures were heading her way.

Pepper Burruss, the Packers' head trainer, had given us some bacteria cream, and that's what Tina and I used to clean ourselves, rubbing it all over our bodies and faces. You couldn't drink the water, so we used bottled water to brush our teeth.

The room had no air-conditioning, of course. It didn't have a fan. The temperature must have been around eighty degrees. I wore the nice blue pajamas that British Airways gave me for our flight to England and cut the sleeves off. We were told to tuck ourselves into the mosquito netting that hung over the bed.

We had to leave the window open, which allowed the mosquitoes to come in, and also the lizards. Tina and I were scrunched into our bed together.

It was so hot, I was sweating profusely.

"What the hell did we get ourselves into?" I asked her.

She burst out laughing.

I couldn't sleep, so I got up and went to find Aaron and Linde Kampman to see how they were doing.

Linde was clinging to Aaron, a 275-pound All-Pro defensive lineman, and she appeared to be crying.

On the floor of her room was a spider about the size of my stretched-out hand. Aaron had stepped on it, but it wouldn't die. It kept moving. He had to keep pounding it to finally kill it.

The next day we met with the tribal leaders. They told us they needed wells for water. All they talked about was how much water they needed. There was no rain in Mutombo, they said, except when there's a deluge. They had systems to collect water, but they were primitive, made of bricks or rocks, and didn't work very well. The water they had was dirty.

"Why don't you use plastic?" I asked.

Turns out, they don't have plastic in Mutombo. They didn't have the resources we take for granted back home.

I met the chief of the tribe in his office. He was in his forties, and he was surrounded by men in army fatigues. I noticed that the chief had air-conditioning and ceiling fans in his office.

The chief was excited to see us at first, interested in talking to us.

"Why are you here?" he wanted to know. "Are you going to help out?"

We told him we were sent by the World Vision organization on a fact-finding mission.

"We're here to look at your situation," we said. "We aren't promising anything."

Immediately his entire attitude changed. He wanted us to understand what he needed from us and he made it clear he expected to get it.

Aaron and Linde Kampman and Troy Murphy and his

wife are white, and the chief refused to even acknowledge they were in the room. Tina and I are African American, and he talked to us a bit, though I could tell from his stern facial expression that what he wanted most was for us to leave.

There are no rules to protect visitors in Kenya. I had heard from the World Vision people things like "Don't make the chief mad. He can make you disappear." And it didn't matter that we came from the United States.

The chief allowed us to take pictures with him at his desk, but he bristled when he was asked to take one outside. He was in a suit, and he was sweating, and after the picture was snapped, he hastily shook our hands and went back inside to the air-conditioning.

"Hey, you guys," I said to the others, "let's get out of here."

We stayed two nights, not for the planned four. Since we weren't able to do anything for these people on our trip, there was no point arranging future meetings with their leaders.

On the second day we met with Africans who had AIDS. We went to a school for the deaf and handed out soccer balls and air pumps. We met widows who lost their husbands in the civil war. These women had come together and built their own farms. The city of Mutombo gave them watermelon seeds, and because water was so scarce and farming so difficult, the melons they grew were considered a delicacy.

They insisted we accept four of the melons as a gift. We at first declined to accept their generosity, because it seemed such an imposition considering how little they had, but they said that to refuse would be very rude and disrespectful. These women were inspirational.

We met one beautiful little girl. In bare feet she was coming to a water well, where the villagers had to buy their water. She had two big buckets on her head that she held steady with two hands and several others strapped to the donkey she was traveling with.

She didn't go to school, she told me, because her family couldn't afford it. She had to work instead, and her job was to leave home every morning and walk for six hours to get water. Then she had to walk back six hours, though it often took longer because she was carrying the water on her head.

"Do you know how beautiful you are?" Tina asked her.

She didn't. She had never seen herself in a mirror.

Tina took her picture and showed it to her. She smiled a beautiful smile. She was twelve years old.

Tina and I wanted to take her home. At least we wanted to help her collect the water and carry the full buckets home.

"Let me help you with that," I said.

She dropped the buckets and stepped back.

"No, sir, please, please, don't touch, sir," she said.

I didn't understand.

"What's wrong?" I asked.

One of the World Vision employees came over and explained to me that men were watching her, and in the Kenyan culture no man is supposed to help a woman. The women do all the work and the labor while the men go out and find jobs and make the money.

These guys are just going to watch her? I thought as my blood began to boil. But I could see the guards watching me.

I stepped back and apologized to the barefoot little girl.

185

She picked up her buckets, strapped them on the donkey, put one on her head, carried another, and started to walk away. She looked back at me and smiled one last time.

We drove back to Nairobi, and we decided to walk the slums. We were told that of the three million people living there, 2.7 million lived in the slums. A guide led us on a tour. He took us to a church where all the kids played soccer. The hope was several of them would be good enough players to be able to leave. The trade-off was that they had to learn to become Christians.

We had to make sure not to walk in the streets, because the speeding cars didn't slow down for anybody. Tina and I looked African, and no one bothered us. No one figured us for Americans until I ran into this one guy, who pointed to me.

"Football," he said. "I watch you on TV."

"That's right," I said.

"Number four," he said. "You quarterback."

"Brett Favre," I said.

He eventually figured it out. He had watched us on ESPN in Nairobi.

"Wow, Drive," Kampman said, "he knew you all the way over here in Africa."

This man pointed to his shirt. It was a Packers shirt that commemorated our winning the Super Bowl the year we lost to Denver. It turned out the clothing manufacturer prints up championship shirts for both teams, and then they send the shirts of the losing team to Nairobi and other cities in Africa. As we were driving toward Mutombo, I saw a man wearing Frank Winters's number 52 jersey.

On the plane ride home I said to Tina, "We are so spoiled. These people have no laws, no rules. We live in freedom to do as we wish. We are so lucky."

What I took away from this trip was that the people we met had nothing. They were living off nickels and dimes. They didn't even have decent drinking water. And yet they were smiling every day.

Now whenever I get in a cab I ask the driver, "Where are you from?"

If he answers he's from Nigeria or Kenya, I tell him how much I respect his people.

"You live every day happy, like there's nothing wrong," I'd say.

In the United States we complain all the time about little things. We complain if we get the wrong kind of cereal in the morning or if we don't have 4G on our phones. Those people we met in Africa were just happy to be alive.

Scott Wells, for a long time the Packers' center, adopted three kids from Africa. He was a St. Louis Ram in 2012, and I can remember his kids running around the field before the game when we played them. I can't help but think how different their lives are because of Scott and his wife. It's pretty awesome.

I RETURNED FROM our trip raring to begin another football season. Aaron played well in 2008, but our substandard 6-10 record overshadowed his accomplishments. Then, in 2009 everyone began to realize that he could really play. He threw for 4,434 yards, just a few yards short of Lynn Dickey's Packers record of 4,458 passing yards in a season.

We were loaded at receiver in 2009. We had five guys who could have started on any NFL team. Greg Jennings and I started. Our backups, Jordy Nelson and James Jones, contributed regularly. At tight end we featured Jermichael Finley and Donald Lee.

Using our West Coast offense we often would have five wide-outs lined up across the field. Coach McCarthy was the mastermind of the offense and the playbook, and it was his decision to challenge the defense this way. We went out there with a swagger. *Stop one of us, and another one of us is going to kill you,* is the way we approached the game. When we walked out on that field, our opponent knew they were facing a tough challenge.

I led our group that year with seventy catches and six touchdown catches. In 2009 I became the tenth player in Packers history to catch fifty touchdown passes in a career when I caught a TD against the Baltimore Ravens. It was my eighth season catching at least fifty or more passes, a franchise record. At thirty-four years of age, I was also the oldest player on the team. Despite having the support of Coach McCarthy and of Aaron Rodgers, I was starting to feel my age. I had been playing on almost crippled knees. After the season I had surgery on both of them.

We finished the 2009 season 11-5, second place in the division. It wasn't supposed to end that way. We had mapped out our road all the way to the Super Bowl—to make it we had to win in domed stadiums. One of those stadiums was in

Phoenix, and in the season finale we went up against another high-scoring team, the Arizona Cardinals, in a game in which Aaron really showed his greatness despite our not winning it.

The game was a shoot-out. Our defense was rated second in the league, but Arizona quarterback Kurt Warner played an excellent game and shredded us.

The game started poorly for us. Aaron threw an interception during our first series of plays, and they scored on a drive. We got the ball back, and Aaron threw me a bubble screen. I caught the ball in the middle of the field and took off downfield. I would have had a touchdown, but one of the Arizona linebackers stripped the ball and it fell out of my arm. Ryan Grant dove for it but missed it completely, and their defense recovered. Arizona scored to take a 14–0 lead.

On the sidelines Aaron brought us all together.

"We just need to keep our composure," he said. "Relax, and let's just play some football."

We were behind 31–10, but after that we made an amazing run, scoring on our next five drives to tie the game 45–45 in regulation.

For overtime we won the coin toss and chose to receive. All we had to do was take the ball down the field and score, we knew, and the Super Bowl would be ours to play in. We just knew we were going to win the game.

On the third play of the overtime Aaron was holding on to the ball, waiting for someone to get open, but Arizona cornerback Michael Adams hit him and he fumbled. The ball came loose and bounced into the arms of linebacker Karlos Dansby, who ran seventeen yards for the winning score.

We lost 51–45. Our season was over.

In the locker room after the game each of us had that look of disbelief on our faces. How could we have lost? The road to victory was simple: All we had to do was go down the field and score in overtime against a team we knew we could score against. And we didn't do it.

For the third time in my career I sat in front of my locker thinking about a Super Bowl in our grasps that wasn't going to be.

Even so, I could see that we were improving, that 2010 was going to be a season I didn't want to miss.

CHAPTER 11

AT

LAST

THE YEAR 2010 was marked by a series of injuries that plagued the Packers from beginning to end. Fifteen of our players were placed on injured reserve. Our star running back Ryan Grant went down in the first game of the season against Philadelphia and missed almost the entire season, and we wondered who was going to fill his shoes. Rookie James Starks, who started the year on the physically unable to perform list, filled in very nicely, it turned out.

Tight end Jermichael Finley went down, and he was replaced by Andrew Quarless and Tom Crabtree. Andrew and Tom filled in admirably.

Among our starters, linebacker Nick Barnett, tackle Mark Tauscher, safety Morgan Burnett, linebacker Brady Poppinga, linebacker Brad Jones, and linebacker Brandon Chillar all were lost for the entire year.

I wasn't immune. In week eight against the New York Jets I tore my quadriceps muscle.

My quad had been hurting for the last couple of weeks. Our trainers knew one of the New York Yankee trainers, and he came over and gave me treatment. He did a great job of getting the knot out right before the Jets game.

I felt good, and we were playing well, and the next thing I knew, I was running down the middle of the field and I popped it. My quad and leg became so stiff I couldn't run, and I was so upset, because I knew I had the opportunity to help the team to a sensational year.

I was on the sidelines, and coach came over and asked me, "Donald, why did you switch the play with Greg?"

"I wanted to see whether they were going to double-team me or double Greg," I said.

After our conversation I could feel my quad get tight. It was completely locked up, and I couldn't move, and there was nothing I could do about it.

I finally had to admit to the trainers, "I may have to have something done."

The doc came over.

"You're done," he said.

I was in great pain just getting onto the plane at LaGuardia Airport to fly back to Green Bay. During the flight it hurt so much I had to keep getting out of my seat to stretch it and try to get it to loosen up.

The next week we were getting ready to play Dallas, and I did all I could to get better so I could play. Meanwhile, the trainer was telling me I would most likely be out six weeks, that there was no way I could come back sooner.

"I'll take off the Dallas game," I told him, "and we have a bye the following week, and I will be back after that."

The team doctor said there was no way.

I missed the next game against Dallas, a game we won 45–7. Aaron threw two touchdown passes to Brandon Jackson, one to Greg Jennings, and one to James Jones. I stood on the sidelines resolved that I would be playing in two weeks.

During our bye week I was injected with a substance called PRP. The doctor takes blood from some other part of your body, separates the red blood cells from the white blood cells, and puts the while blood cells back inside your body. It's something everyone in college and the pros does now. It's amazing. It was something new, and I didn't think it was going to work, but I was willing to try it. Doc thought it would work, but he didn't think I'd recover as fast as I did. I had two injections, and after the bye week, I was ready to play. I came back to play the rest of the season.

Aaron even missed a game after he suffered a concussion against the Detroit Lions. Our next game was against the New England Patriots, away, and without Aaron we figured that his backup, Matt Flynn, had to be about perfect if we were going to beat the Patriots.

Flynn, who led LSU to a national championship in 2008, was amazing. He was 24 for 37 for 251 yards and three touchdowns in a 31–27 loss. One spectacular TD was a sixty-six-yarder from Flynn to James Jones. At the end of the game Matt threw an interception to give the Pats possession, and Tom Brady made a gutsy call and threw for a touchdown to beat us as time ran out.

Despite Flynn's great play, there was a lot of grousing in the locker room after the game. A couple of our receivers were complaining about not getting the ball thrown to them enough.

I was sick of it. I got up and said, "Stop worrying about how many balls you catch. Just focus on winning."

The frustration, especially after all the injuries, was getting to us. With two games to go, our record was only 8–6, and with another loss, we faced elimination from the playoffs.

To reach the wild card we needed to defeat two excellent teams, the New York Giants and the Chicago Bears. After that Patriots loss, every game to the end would be do-or-die.

I did what I could to keep everyone upbeat.

"We spend so much time looking at the door that's about to close that we forget the door that's about to open," I said, quoting Alexander Graham Bell, the inventor of the telephone. It was trite, but it was true. The players filling in for our injured guys were doing a very good job.

Against the Giants Aaron completed 25 for 37 passes for 404 yards and four touchdowns. Eli Manning threw four interceptions. We cruised to a 45–17 win. The star for us was fullback John Kuhn, a Pittsburgh Steelers reject who caught a touchdown pass and ran for three more.

We next had to face the Chicago Bears, not an easy team to beat. With an 11-4 record, they had run away with the NFL North division title.

Before the game I was talking with Bears safety Chris Harris. I suggested that he be nice to us.

"You know," he said, "we're not going to let you guys into the playoffs."

The game was a defensive struggle. There was no score the first quarter, the Bears kicked a field goal in the second period, and we kicked one in the third to tie the game at 3 apiece. In the fourth quarter, after Aaron hit me for a twenty-one-yard gain, he threw a deep post to Greg Jennings for forty-six yards. Greg was pushed out of bounds at the one.

Aaron then threw a one-yard touchdown pass to our tight end Donald Lee to win it.

Needing a touchdown, Bears quarterback Jay Cutler threw deep to Devin Hester, but the pass was intercepted by our Nick Collins. The win put us in the playoffs. After all those injuries, it really was a minor miracle.

IN THE PLAYOFFS we were the sixth, and lowest, seed. All of our games would have to be played on the road. No team in Super Bowl history had ever overcome such odds to win it all.

I was a twelve-year veteran in 2010. Only three other players on the Packers team had ten years of experience—Charles Woodson, Chad Clifton, and Ryan Pickett. In the locker room before the playoffs, I told my team, "We've got to win it now. This is it for me. I want to win the Super Bowl now, because next year isn't certain. There's only one chance to get this thing. Don't be thinking *Oh, I got next year.* I can tell you from being in this league a long time, next year isn't promised to you."

Our journey to the Super Bowl came down to three road games. The first was in Philadelphia, a team we had defeated in the first week of the season. Aaron was terrific, throwing three touchdown passes to Tom Crabtree, James Jones, and Brandon Jackson. I had five catches for fifty-six yards, including one play when I ran a deep cross down the sideline on third down, splitting two defenders just as Aaron threw the ball. It was an important first down on the way to a touchdown.

Michael Vick, the Eagles quarterback, threw for almost three hundred yards but only one touchdown. He was moving the Eagles down the field at the end of the fourth quarter when our cornerback, Tramon Williams, made an incredible interception in the end zone with thirty-six seconds left in the game. David Akers, who beat us in overtime to crush our chances of going to the Super Bowl in 2003, missed two field goals. Karma, baby, karma.

FOOTBALL HAS BEEN an important part of my life, but in November 2010 I was reminded that there are times when football has to take a backseat. Bryant Pretlow had been a dear friend of mine since college. He had played basketball for Alcorn State, and we were close like brothers. We would share clothing— even though he was a lot bigger than I was. He was six foot six and would wear size XL, but back then I liked to wear my clothes big and baggy, and he'd always lend me his shirts.

He majored in criminal justice, which was Tina's major as well. His girlfriend at the time was in the band with Tina, and it was through Bryant that Tina and I hooked up. Without him, Tina and I never would have been together.

The Saturday night before our game with the Dallas Cowboys, I had gotten a call from Bryant's mom, urging me to come to Norfolk, Virginia, to see him.

"He's not feeling too good," she said. "He might not make it."

He was working in special services in the army, and in our last conversation he had said he was working a lot and was tired. The truth was he had cancer, Hodgkin's disease, and he didn't want to tell me.

His mom was the one who finally told me about the cancer.

After the Dallas game, we had a bye week, and I told him I'd fly in to see him. I was scheduled to fly to Virginia on Wednesday. Another really good friend of mine, Timon Durrett, an actor we called Tree, went to see Bryant on Tuesday afternoon.

Tree arrived first. As he walked into the room to see Bryant, he was talking to me on the phone. Tree screamed at me, "He's gone, Quickie! He's gone!"

I lost it. I burst into tears.

About a half hour later Tree called back. Bryant was breathing again. Bryant's aunt got on the phone.

"Quickie," she said, "Bryant's waiting on you. I told him you were on your way, and he took another breath."

There was a flight leaving Dallas in half an hour for Norfolk. I called the airline and asked them to hold it for me.

"My best friend is passing away, and I need to get there," I said.

I made the flight.

Tree picked me up at the airport.

"He's waiting on you, man," Tree said.

I walked into Bryant's room. His mom, aunts, brother, and girlfriend all were there. He was lying in bed, barely breathing, taking noisy, strained breaths.

"Hey, P," I said. "I'm here, man. If you're ready to go, you can go now."

He was unable to speak.

I moved close to him. He opened his eyes, and as I walked toward him I could see he was following my movements. I grabbed his hand, and he moved a finger.

"Hey, man, you can't go," I started babbling. "We have all these plans. When I retire, we're going to do all these things together for kids in Virginia, give these kids an opportunity. You can't go on me now."

He couldn't talk.

He was having trouble breathing and he wanted to roll over. I picked him up in my arms, and he let out a heavy sigh.

"Hold on, Bryant, just a little longer," I pleaded with him. I told him Tina and the kids would be out the next day to see him.

He took one more breath—and that was it.

Bryant was thirty-five years old. How can you explain that? If that doesn't shake your believe in God, nothing will.

I couldn't accept he was gone. I wouldn't let him go. I lay in the bed with him, holding him, until his mom said, "Quickie, you *have* to let him go."

"He's tired," I said. "He's just sleeping. I'm going to hold him awhile."

I couldn't accept that he had died.

I stayed with him for two hours until the coroners came.

The coroners, Tree, and I picked him up. To the coroners he wasn't anybody—to Tree and me he meant everything.

"He's my best friend," I told the coroners. "Don't treat him like a nobody."

After they made the arrangements the next day, I left for Green Bay. Coach McCarthy said I could leave practice to attend his funeral.

When Bryant passed away, I *felt* cancer. Cancer to me went from being a disease to something much more personal.

When you lose family members to drugs or to gangs, it's terrible, but you have some control over those things. You had a choice. With cancer, there's no choice. That's tough. I had never experienced the feeling of being robbed because someone you love was taken too soon, taken against their will when they had no choice.

Cancer has been on my mind a lot since then. My foundation does so much for homeless families, feeding them and finding them housing, but I have to find a way to add cancer awareness to the list of causes just because of Bryant and the cruel way he died. I just have to.

I returned home with a heavy heart. The top-seeded Atlanta Falcons were next. Earlier in the year we had lost to them 20–17.

Normally before a game we stayed in downtown Atlanta. We would go to Peachtree Street and hit the restaurants and bars and enjoy ourselves. Before this game Coach McCarthy took us waaaaaay out to the woods. I don't even know where we were, what town the hotel was in. It was the boonies.

"Our original designated hotel was already booked," Coach McCarthy told us.

As a result, he said, we had to stay in a hotel in the middle of nowhere.

And I mean nowhere. I felt like I was back at Alcorn State. There was no mall. There was no McDonald's. With nowhere to go and nothing to do, no one even thought of breaking curfew.

James Jones, myself, and a couple other guys were going stir crazy, so I paid one of the hotel employees to hijack one of the hotel vans and take us to McDonald's. On the way I spied a Chick-fil-A.

"Pull over!" I yelled. "We have to eat at Chick-fil-A!"

It's one of my favorite places to eat, but I only get to eat there when I'm in Dallas.

I ordered nuggets, a sandwich, and some fries. After that, there was nothing to do but head back to the hotel.

Mike had wanted to make sure we were focused, and against the Falcons we were just that. We scored forty-eight points, the most the Packers ever scored in a postseason game. We won the game 48–21.

Greg Jennings had 101 receiving yards. Jordy had 79 yards including a touchdown. James Jones had 75 yards and a touchdown catch. One highlight just before the half was an interception and 70-yard touchdown run by cornerback Tramon Williams. We were so far ahead Matt Flynn finished the game.

Our punter, Tim Masthay, never got off the bench.

THERE WAS ONE more game before the Super Bowl. Our opponents were President Barack Obama's Chicago Bears. The last time the Green Bay Packers had faced the Bears in a postseason game was back in 1941, just after Pearl Harbor.

Winning big can sometimes be a trap. After winning big, you say to yourself, *Piece of cake. We can do this every week.* But as I've learned from bitter experience, it doesn't work that way. The next week against a different defense, you can get shut out and then you begin to question your ability. Pro football is a very difficult game, and not just physically.

During the playoffs I worked hard to keep everyone focused on the next opponent.

"We're going to take it one game at a time," I said to the team several times in the locker room. "We're going to beat the guy in front of us, one-on-one, all day long. If we can do that, we'll continue.

"And we have to keep making the plays."

As I sat in the locker room before the game, a couple of the younger players asked me, "Drive, have you ever been to an NFL Championship Game?"

"I've been to one," I told them, "against the Giants in 2007. We lost that game, so I know what losing an NFL Championship Game feels like. The biggest thing is, we have to win and get to the Super Bowl. That's my goal, to get to that game. I dream of this. I've been dreaming of this for a *long* time." The game was a seesaw affair, more a war than a game. When the final whistle blew, we came away with a 21–14 win, a victory that started with a one-yard touchdown run by Aaron and then a four-yard touchdown run by James Starks, our rookie find, and after the Bears scored, B. J. Raji, our young nose tackle, intercepted a Caleb Hanie pass and ran it eighteen yards for a touchdown to make it 21–7. Hanie managed a touchdown pass late in the fourth quarter, but time ran out on the Bears as we became the first sixth-seeded playoff team to go to a Super Bowl. As I sat there after the game I thought about the tremendous job that general manager Ted Thompson had done to put the team together. I was one of the few players who were already on the team when he arrived. Most all of the Packers were his handpicked choices.

I couldn't believe it.

We were going to the Super Bowl.

I held the NFC Championship trophy in my hands, and I was kissing it. I thought, *In the next couple of weeks I hope to hold the Vince Lombardi Trophy and kiss that, too.*

CHAPTER 12

THE
RING

MY OFF-SEASON HOME is in Flower Mound, Texas, and so no one was more delighted than I to be playing in Super Bowl XLV in Dallas, twenty miles away. Playing near home didn't distract me at all. It made me more comfortable. You might think that pro athletes are blasé about things like this, but I was living out a dream—playing in the Super Bowl in my backyard. It wasn't in Houston, my hometown, but it was close enough. I was able to bring some forty family members to the game without having to fly them in. They were all able to come to Dallas and celebrate with me.

I thought it ironic that though we were playing in the South, in the days before the game not only was it freezing, with temperatures in the teens, but a weather system dumped snow all over the Dallas metropolitan area. The freeways and interstates were abandoned and empty. In the suburbs Texans slipped and slided on unplowed streets.

We were watching the pregame interviews on TV in our hotel room when we saw Bryant McFadden, a cornerback for the Steelers, our opponents, trash-talking. He was asked whether he had any fear facing "the best group of receivers in the NFL."

I'll admit it was a stupid question, but McFadden decided to be a wiseguy.

"Yeah, I'm afraid," he said. "I should just go back to the hotel, pack my bag, get back on the plane, and go back to Pittsburgh." Then he started to laugh.

James Jones, for one, took his comment personally.

"You're not going to give us any credit on national TV!" James shouted at the TV set. "We'll show you!"

And that's exactly what we did.

In front of 103,000 fans at Cowboys Stadium, the first time the Super Bowl ever was played there, Aaron got us started with a twenty-nine-yard touchdown pass to Jordy. Our talented safety Nick Collins then intercepted a Ben Roethlisberger pass and returned it thirty-seven yards for a touchdown. We led 14–0. I had two catches and was feeling optimistic about things when at the end of the second quarter I suffered a severely sprained ankle and had to leave the game.

I ran a stick route—I was supposed to run five yards, catch the ball, and take off. Aaron got me the ball, and as I started to turn upfield, James Harrison, the Steelers middle linebacker, jumped on my back and dragged me down. My leg, knee, and ankle got all twisted around as I fell. I was in so much pain I don't know how I was able to hold on to the ball.

"Drive, are you okay?" Harrison asked.

I shook my head no.

Everything was hurting as I limped to the sidelines.

All I could think about was getting back into the game.

This will have to calm down soon, I thought.

As I lay on the X-ray table, I heard someone say, "Oh my God, Charles is on his way in."

Woodson had suffered a shoulder injury.

"What's wrong with Wood?" was the reply.

Charles Woodson was our Pro Bowl safety. In 2009 he was the NFL defensive player of the year. He had played in a Super Bowl for the Oakland Raiders, but he had been hurt and not at full strength, and the Raiders lost. This was Charles's Super Bowl quest, much as it was mine.

I sat on the X-ray table with ice on my ankle and knee. Wood came in holding his shoulder and looking fighting mad. He walked past me without saying anything and went into one of the other X-ray rooms. Then I heard crashing. Wood was tearing up the room, throwing objects, kicking things around. He had seen the X-rays. His collarbone was broken.

I could hear our team doctor Patrick McKenzie telling our head trainer Pepper Burrus, "Someone has to tell him he can't play."

That's brutal, I thought.

I felt awful for Charles. This is what he dreamed about— *dreamed about*—getting back to the Super Bowl and winning it.

"Someone's got to tell him," the doc said again.

I kept thinking they were talking about Wood. But Wood already knew.

They were talking about me.

Doc and Pepper came over to tell me my day was done.

"Can't you tape me up, like you did for the Seattle game?" I asked them.

"Flea," I said to our trainer, Bryan Engel, "remember that tape job?"

He nodded yes.

Flea taped my ankle. I stood up. All I could feel was intense pain.

"I feel good," I lied.

"Jump," said Doc McKenzie.

"I'm good," I said. "I don't need to jump."

"Jump," he insisted. "Jump for me."

I couldn't. I couldn't even take a tiny hop.

"I can't," I had to admit. "I'm in too much pain."

Desperate to return, I begged them to inject my ankle with cortisone.

"Anything," I pleaded. "Something. Put me in a walking cast. I've got to play. This is what I dreamed of."

It was halftime when receiver Greg Jennings walked in. Earlier I had sworn to him that I was okay, that I would be ready for the second half. I sat on the table with my head down.

Greg came over and hugged me. Doc didn't have the heart to speak the words that would tell me I couldn't play, but Greg and I both knew.

My eyes began to water. I couldn't stop myself from crying.

The other receivers were patting me on the back, telling me not to get down.

"We're going to win this game for you, Drive," they said.

Before every game our little group of receivers would gather together and huddle, and we'd chant, "One, two, three wide-outs." Before they went out for the second half of the Super Bowl, they gathered around me and together we chanted, "One, two, three wide-outs."

They left, leaving me in the locker room desolate and alone. Depressed, I figured I'd get dressed and sit alone in the locker room during the second half of the game. I could no longer contribute, and it hurt too much just to stand there and watch.

Doc and Pepper wouldn't allow it.

"They need you out there," they said. "The only way they're going to win this game is to have you out there. You can contribute by coaching and cheerleading the guys."

They put me in a boot so I wouldn't have to go out there with crutches.

As I limped from the locker room out onto the Cowboys Stadium field, I looked up at the huge jumbotron that hovered above. We were leading 21–10.

On third down Aaron threw a pass to James Jones, who had the defender beat. Had he caught it, he would have had a touchdown. But he dropped it.

The Steelers scored again to pull to within four, at 21–17.

"Come on, J.J.!" I was screaming on the sidelines.

I talked to James. Everyone talked to James. To win we needed him to focus and catch the ball. After a couple of passes that Jordy didn't catch, I did the same thing with him.

All the receivers came together on the sidelines.

"Go back to the basics," I said. "Focus and catch the ball." I said it in an encouraging way with a sense of urgency.

James wanted to know why everyone was on his case.

I didn't say a word.

"You know what to do," I told him. "Now go do it."

We were leading 21–17 going into the fourth quarter. On third down Jordy made an unbelievable grab for thirty-eight yards, his longest catch of the game. He almost dove in for a touchdown, which would have been his second of the night.

It was at that point that I thought, *We're going to win this game. These boys are going to do it.*

Greg Jennings caught a touchdown to put us ahead 28–17, and after he caught the ball he started pointing to his finger. I wondered whether he had dislocated it, but that wasn't it at all. Greg was referring back to the night before when we were fitted for our Super Bowl rings.

On the sidelines when he was asked what he was doing, Greg said, "I was putting on my Super Bowl ring."

That's when I *knew* we were going to win.

That night we defeated Pittsburgh 31–25. After Mason Crosby kicked a field goal, our defense kept the Steelers from scoring as time ran out. Aaron Rodgers, who threw for 304 yards and three touchdowns and who rewarded Coach McCarthy's confidence in his ability to replace Brett Favre, was named the Super Bowl MVP.

When the final whistle blew I didn't feel cheated in any way, even though I was too injured to play in the second half. It would have been different if I hadn't played at all. If I hadn't played, people might have questioned whether I deserved a ring. But I had two catches for twenty-eight yards, so I contributed something, and I was satisfied, even happy to play a role in the Packers' fourth Super Bowl victory in its history.

After the game was over I sat in the locker room with the other Packers players. Greg, Jordy, James Jones, Bryan Bulaga, Josh Sitton, and Ryan Taylor were sitting around me. I couldn't help it, but I was crying. I couldn't contain my emotions.

"Thank you, guys," I said. "I appreciate this. After thirteen years I'm finally getting my opportunity to be a champion. I owe it to everyone in this locker room."

The young players were looking at me as if to say, *This is your first one?*

They were thinking that they'd have plenty of opportunities to win a Super Bowl, but if you're in the league long enough, you come to understand just how difficult it is. Usually it's once in a lifetime. Not too many NFL football players even have the opportunity to play in the game.

WINNING THE SUPER Bowl was also a thrill for Tina and the kids. When we first came to Green Bay, I told Tina, "I will never attend a Super Bowl game until I'm in one. In fact, I will never watch one on TV until I'm in one."

"That doesn't make any sense," she said to me.

But it was how I felt about it. I refused to go. I refused to watch—until we beat the Steelers. And every year after that I've watched the games knowing I was a Super Bowl champion.

My son, Cristian, was excited as well. He knew it had always been his daddy's dream to play in a Super Bowl game. My boy was happy for me.

We had a ring ceremony in Green Bay. Charles Woodson and I had our pictures taken together with our rings. Our entire careers—twenty-five years of NFL football between us—was all for that ring. No one can ever take that away from us.

My ring is in a safe.

A lot of people have told me that it would have been acceptable, even understandable, if I had retired right then. I was badly injured. I had won a Super Bowl, a storybook ending for a lowly seventh-round draft pick.

That thought never entered my mind.

When you win one, you want another.

AFTER WE DEFEATED Barack Obama's Bears in the NFC Championship at Soldier Field and won the Super Bowl, we were invited to the White House as world champions. The first player President Obama hugged was me. Greg Jennings, who was standing behind us, wanted to know if everyone was going to get a hug.

"Donald and I go back a long way," President Obama said. "We're probably the same age, right Donald?"

"No," I said, "you're a little bit older than I am."

It was very neat, very special.

When I look back at our Super Bowl victory, what I think about most is just how difficult it is to get there. You always think it's going to happen, but then year after year, it doesn't, so when you finally play in the game, you appreciate the atmosphere and everything that comes with it, the festivities, the throng of press, and buildup—I embraced everything about it. The other thing I love: I have a Super Bowl trophy and a Super Bowl ring in my house that I will cherish forever.

AFTER OUR SUPER Bowl win in February 2011, the owners locked us NFL players out. We had no collective bargaining agreement, and there were labor issues to resolve. We had to stay away from our teams.

I had messed up my medial collateral ligament (MCL) as well as my lateral collateral ligament (LCL) in my left knee on that play. The doctors gave me a boot to wear to take the pressure off my swollen foot. I wore it for almost two months.

When it appeared that the NFL owners and the NFL Players Association couldn't agree on anything, on my own and without telling anyone I went ahead and had an operation on my hip. For years my hip had pinched me. Every time I planted my foot or came out of a break I felt the pain. Sometimes when I stretched, the hip joint would pop. I played on it anyway.

Dr. Thomas Byrd, my hip doctor, said that because I wasn't able to twist and move the right way, I was overworking the other muscles. He said that's why I had popped a quad muscle. Cartilage had formed over the bone, and he cleaned that up.

After the hip surgery, whenever I did a promotional or public appearance, I would come on crutches but then put them aside and hide them. I was on crutches for six weeks. It wasn't too long before the pain in my hip was gone. I could run and cut again.

I had been badly hurt in the Super Bowl, and I knew I had to get my body back in shape. I felt it was important to keep the hip surgery from the public because at the age of thirty-six, if the press and public knew I had had my hip operated on in addition to the other procedures, questions concerning my ability to play would come fast and furious. Over and over I would have to answer questions like "How long can you still play? Are you declining?"

If I had been younger and had the surgeries, no one would have questioned it. I would have come back, felt amazing, and that would have been the end of it. But when you're older . . .

My new goal was to play until I was forty. That, and to go to another Super Bowl.

THE LOCKOUT ENDED on the eve of training camp. The Packers came back to Green Bay heavily favored to repeat as Super Bowl champions.

The most games the Packers had ever won in a season was thirteen. In 2011 we began the season 13-0.

We finished the year with a stellar 15-1 record. Our only loss was to the Kansas City Chiefs in a huge upset. There is only one team in NFL history to go undefeated through the league championship, and that was the 1972 Miami Dolphins. We so badly wanted to be the second team to do that, but on any given Sunday you can lose, and that's what happened to us against Kansas City.

It was a terrible loss, because we knew we didn't play our best ball. Kansas City should not have beaten us. They were not a good team, but when you have a great team that doesn't play as well as it should, then you lose. To go undefeated we had to play great every time we stepped onto that field, and on this day we didn't do it.

But the loss to Kansas City was the turning point of our season because after that we decided, *Okay, we can't take teams lightly anymore. We're going to have to put our feet on a team's throat in games,* and that's what we started to do toward the end of the season. After that loss, we started putting teams away.

In the first quarter of that game I broke my middle finger again. I reached down to catch a ball on third and twelve, running a twenty-yard route, and as I turned for the ball, Aaron threw it close to the ground. I probably shouldn't have reached for it, but I've always caught with my hands, so I reached down, and as I was tackled, the next thing I heard was a crack. I dropped the ball for an incomplete pass, and ran to the sidelines.

"Are you okay, Drive?" asked the trainer.

"Yeah, I'm okay," I lied.

I knew my finger was broken. Later in the game I went back in and caught the only Packers touchdown in the game.

After the game was over I took my glove off and went back to see the trainer.

"You broke your finger when?" he wanted to know.

"The first quarter."

"Why didn't you tell me?"

"Because you'd have pulled me out if I had told you."

WE EARNED A first-round bye. After a week off we returned to prepare for the New York Giants in the playoffs. We had played the Giants during the regular season and just beat them. Aaron and Eli Manning had had a shoot-out. Aaron, who threw me two beautiful touchdown passes, won it. Clay Matthews, our star linebacker, intercepted Manning and ran the ball back thirty-eight yards for a touchdown, and with the score tied 35–35 with three seconds left, Mason Crosby coolly kicked a thirty-one-yard field goal to win it for us. We were sure the rematch in the playoffs would be just as tough.

As we returned to work, the Packers were struck by tragedy. Joe Philbin was our offensive coordinator, and for a day and a half his twenty-one-year-old son Michael had gone missing. Later there was a police report that early on a cold Sunday morning a man who had fallen through the ice in Fox River was crying out for help. We held out hope it wasn't Joe's son, but it was.

Why Michael was out on the thin ice in January in the middle of the night was a mystery. A student at Ripon College, Michael had spent Saturday night bar-hopping, and his friends thought he was heading back to the university. He never made it.

Coach Philbin left the team to be with his family and prepare for Michael's funeral, which was on a Friday in Green Bay, two days before our playoff game with the Giants. It was tough. Joe and I had been friends. We had been together since 2003, when he began as the assistant line coach; he had quickly moved up to offensive coordinator. I knew Michael since he was a child.

Joe was the mastermind behind our offense, a guy with bright ideas. He'd write down plays on a napkin during dinner and show them to us the next day. He was one of the few coaches whom Mike McCarthy kept on the staff after Mike Sherman was fired.

He had a play to beat any coverage. He had a play for me

called the flanker short post. I'd come in motion, and I'd split the linebackers real quick, and Brett or Aaron would throw me the ball. It was always a catch for me.

I loved to needle Joe.

"You need to put more plays in for number eighty," I'd tell him.

"You have plenty of plays," he'd say.

To get a call that your child is gone is devastating. We got a lot of questions about whether we were going to dedicate the Giants playoff game to Joe and Michael. How do you answer that? Most of the guys didn't even know Michael. Hell, most of them didn't really know Joe.

"I want to win for Joe," I said.

I wanted to repeat what we had done the year before.

But I had another problem. My age. In 2011 the reporters wouldn't let it go. I never should have read the papers. If I hadn't I wouldn't have seen the doubters talking about my reduced playing time, how I had gone from six straight seasons of 70 or more catches for 1,000 yards to 51 catches in 2010 for 565 yards and 37 catches in 2011 for 445 yards.

At the start of the season they wondered whether I had lost my speed, but then against the Detroit Lions in November I had caught a pass from Matt Flynn in the middle, split the two defenders, and outrun everyone for a touchdown. That ended that debate.

Then I scored those two touchdowns against the Giants in the regular season. I caught one in the back of the end zone because they let me go. The second touchdown was scored in front of Corey Webster, a top cornerback. I caught it falling out of bounds. After the game the reporters were lavishing me with praise, calling me "twinkle toes," which made me laugh because not long before that they were trying to bury me, pointing out that my numbers were declining.

I wanted to tell them it had nothing to do with my having less skill, but as it was with Brett, it came down to age. Once you turn thirty, everyone starts asking, *Can you still play?* All you can do is try to prove everyone wrong.

But I couldn't get away from reporters asking about my reduced playing time. Hell, I was on a team with some truly great receivers like Greg Jennings, Jordy Nelson, James Jones, Jermichael Finley, and Randall Cobb. These were first-class weapons.

I answered my critics when in the second-round playoff game against the Giants I had three catches for forty-five yards and a touchdown. With those catches I was able to set a Packers record for most postseason receptions with 49. My 675 career yards in playoff games is second in Packers history.

Unfortunately, we played a terrible game against the Giants. We did the same thing in the playoff game that we did against Kansas City that year. We didn't finish. We dropped balls. We didn't execute on special teams. We didn't execute on offense. And we lost.

Eli Manning threw three touchdown passes, while our receivers dropped a total of nine passes. We also had four turnovers, including an interception. Why we were so bad will forever be a mystery, though the critics focused on the fact that Coach McCarthy had rested his starters in the final game against the Detroit Lions. Aaron went a full three weeks without taking the field.

One difference was that I didn't play as much in the playoff game against the Giants as I did in the regular season game against them. As you get older you start asking yourself, *Why aren't I playing as much?* I just couldn't wrap my finger around that. I was having a good year, and then boom, I didn't play much in the most important game of the year.

At the end of the game it was *We have to step up*, and they put the Old Man in. I was put in the game late in the third quarter against the Giants, and I caught everything, including for a touchdown. It just wasn't enough. We didn't have enough time left on the clock. We ran out of time. That's what got us in the end.

The 37–20 loss to the Giants at Lambeau Field was terribly deflating. Here we had posted a 15-1 record, the best in Packers history, but what did it matter if we couldn't get past the second round of the playoffs? Who among the Packers fans cared that the Giants themselves would go on to win the Super Bowl?

Not one.

It was going to be a long winter—until show business came a-calling.

CHAPTER 13

DANCING WITH THE STARS

AFTER OUR SON, Cristian, was born, we didn't do any family planning. Whatever happened was going to happen, and Tina became pregnant again. She started spotting, and the doctors were sure she was going to have a miscarriage. She was ordered to do bed rest, and she did that, and in 2005, twenty-three months after Cristian was born, I was blessed with the most beautiful girl in the world, Christina.

"I don't want any more kids," I told Tina, and I was serious about that.

I was blessed with two.

Tina understood, but every once in a while she'd say, "Just one more."

One night we went to a Bible retreat for pro athletes with Packers defensive lineman Ryan Pickett and his wife, Jennifer; and another teammate, defensive tackle Colin Cole, and his wife, Kay. For whatever reason, on the last night of the retreat I said to Tina, "I'm okay if you want to have another baby."

She was so excited.

She told Jennifer and Kay what I had said.

The pregnancy was easy and smooth. Tina worked out a lot and stayed in great shape. Our daughter Charity was born right before the first game of the 2011 season against the New Orleans Saints. Coach McCarthy allowed me to stay in the hospital with my family.

How many blessings can I get? I asked myself when I looked at Charity.

I realized that when God said "Be fruitful," He meant it in a special way. To bring kids into the world is a gift. It makes you a better person by having them. You learn what matters most in your life.

Everyone figures that because I play football, the sport is the most important thing in my life. I breathe, sleep, and eat football. I love the game, but I live for my family. When I'm home, people ask me, "Are you watching football on TV?" I don't, and it doesn't matter who's playing or winning. When I'm home I turn off the TV and play with my wife and kids.

You don't find many men who come home at night from a hard day's work and want to play with the kids or help clean up the house. I do that. It's a legacy from when my mom used to clean hotel rooms. If the kitchen is a mess after Tina cooks, I clean it up. I can put the babies to bed as easily as she can. I try not to add any burdens to her life if I can help it.

I had a ritual before every home game with my family. Cristian, Christina, Charity, Tina, I, and whoever else from our family was there, took part. Before I walked out the door to head to Lambeau Field, we all came together and said a prayer.

And whoever wanted to ride with me to the game could.

The fellowship also extended during the ride to the ballpark. I lived in De Pere, ten minutes from the field, and often I got caught up in the traffic snarl trying to enter Lombardi Avenue. I just rolled down my window, found a car or truck with Packers decals all over it, rolled down my window, and asked, "Hey, can I get over!"

The reaction was always the same. They did a double take, their eyes got wide, and they waved me over. The seas parted, and I drove right to the stadium.

I've never had any dreams about what I was going to do after football. I had a singular focus: It was always football, football, football.

"You can go on and do anything," my friend and agent Brian Lammi said to me. "You can be a commentator on ESPN. You can be a coach."

I wasn't sure I had it in me to become an analyst on a TV sports channel full-time. I also didn't think I wanted to be a coach.

When Brian asked me what I wanted to do, I said, "Nothing. I want to sit at home, relax, and know that I've done everything that I could do as a football player."

Then on a Friday in January 2012 I received a phone call from a producer in Hollywood asking if I would be interested in becoming a contestant during the fourteenth season of *Dancing with the Stars*, one of the most popular shows in all of television. The way the show works, twelve professional dancers are paired with celebrities from all walks of life in a dance contest watched by some thirty-five million viewers on TV. Among the celebrities who won in the past were two NFL stars, Emmitt Smith of the Dallas Cowboys and Hines Ward of the Pittsburgh Steelers. Among other athletes who competed and won were the figure skater Kristi Yamaguchi, speed skater Apolo Anton Ohno, and Formula 1 race car driver Helio Castroneves. Other winners included the singer Donny Osmond and the actress Jennifer Grey, the star of *Dirty Dancing*. I've been a longtime fan of the show, and I wasn't surprised that Jennifer won. She and the late Patrick Swayze were absolutely electric in that movie. The girl can dance.

I sat down with Tina and my kids Christina, six, and Cristian, who was eight. (Charity was six months old.) We had to make a decision literally in a couple of hours. I felt it was a great opportunity for bigger and better things, not just for me, but for Tina and the kids as well.

"We should do it," I said.

But Tina wasn't on board. She didn't want to leave Dallas, where we lived in the off-season, for three and a half months. She didn't want to pull the kids out of school.

"There's a lot of things to think about," she said.

Christina also wasn't on board at first.

"No, daddy," she said. "I don't want you to do it because you will be dancing with another woman."

"Oh Lord," I said, "I was thinking your mom was going to say that—but you said it."

The only member of my family in my corner was eight-year-old Cristian, who said, "Dad, this happens once in a lifetime; you should do it."

Tina finally gave her okay, though very reluctantly. She could see the good it might do for me. But she also saw the angst that my dancing with a beautiful professional dancer might bring to her. In the end she chose to put my feelings first.

"This could be good," she said finally, though I wasn't sure she meant it. Once she was on board, we all crowded around the phone, put it on speaker, and called Brian, my agent and friend.

"Let's do this," I said.

"Yes!" he yelled. "I love you guys!"

I was going on *Dancing with the Stars*. I just didn't know who my dancing partner would be. I was told she would be coming over to my house and introducing herself. It was all so unreal. In football you are one of eleven players on the field. In *Dancing with the Stars* it's just you and your partner putting everything on the line in front of a worldwide audience. In a way the pressure of performing on this show approached the pressure I felt playing in the Super Bowl.

I was sitting on the couch in my living room when the doorbell rang. Tina and the kids started screaming. Tina and I had been watching the show since season one. This was season fourteen. Brian and Tina thought I'd have the best shot at winning if I danced with a partner who had won in the past.

I preferred to dance with an underdog.

I opened the door and greeted professional dancer Peta Murgatroyd, a native of New Zealand.

I can't believe it's Peta, I said to myself. I had hoped it would be someone like her, an underdog who one season lost the championship dancing with NBA star Ron Artest of the Los Angeles Lakers. The season before this one she had been eliminated in the very first round.

I was elated, because I knew she could dance. She had choreographed and performed with great artists including Rod Stewart, Taio Cruz, Enrique Iglesias, and New Kids on the Block. But for most of the time on *Dancing with the Stars* she had been relegated to chorus line status. Victory, I knew, would be so much sweeter if we were underdogs who then went on to win it all.

Peta, blond and shapely, walked into the room, followed by a camera crew, and introduced herself with her heavy New Zealand accent.

"I know who you are," I said.

She asked me if I could dance and I said, "Yeah, I can shake a leg, I can hold my own at a bar, a club, or at a party."

Then I heard, "Cut!" The producer asked us if we would please tape it all over again. It was my welcome to the world of live reality television.

She asked me if I could do the cha-cha.

"Yes, of course."

We went and danced together that first night at a studio in Dallas. When I rolled up my pants legs, she said, "Oh. My. God. You have some of the skinniest legs in this world!"

I acted offended.

"What? Look, these things are strong," I said. "These legs have made me a lot of money."

"You have chicken legs."

That's how the whole relationship started. It was very much a brother-sister relationship. She had a boyfriend, and I was married. We could tease each other and still get our work done.

Tina decided she was going to stay behind in Dallas with the kids. I could see she was very unhappy that I was going away, even unhappier that I was going away to dance with a good-looking woman who was going to teach me how to dance and whom I was going to hold close to me for the next three months.

Tina needn't have worried. If I had wanted to play the field, I wouldn't have gotten married. I tell people, "I married my best friend. I can tell my best friend anything." When I said "I do," I promised to love Tina the way God wanted me to.

Before I met her I was always that guy who said, *If I can get this girl, it would be awesome.* But when I met Tina, that changed. God brought her to me to save my life. I was selling drugs, and without her I would have continued to go down that road. She made me stop, and I owe her everything.

I always told Tina, "You never have to worry about my messing around, because I married you for a reason. It wasn't just your looks. You have everything a man could want."

There are women out there, beautiful women, who want to sleep with you for the adventure of it. There are others who want to do it just so they can call your wife on the phone and ruin your life. Others do it so they can get you to pay their light bill or their rent. And I know guys who have said, "Let's go." And I know other athletes who have had to pay these women so they don't tell their wives. Sometimes the woman messes up the marriage anyway—it's why some of these athletes get divorced.

After I married Tina, I never gave myself the opportunity to give in to temptation. I could be anywhere—a grocery store or a club when I was younger—and a beautiful girl might ask me, "What are you doing tonight?"

I'd tell her right out, "I'm married."

"I know how athletes are," she'd say.

"Let me ask you something," I'd say. "What can you do for me that my wife can't? And don't answer right away. Take your time."

I got different answers.

My answer was always the same: "No, no, no."

I will never say "I do" to another woman. If something ever happened to Tina, I would not remarry. I'm like the swan that mates for life. It's Tina to the final whistle.

TWO DAYS AFTER Peta arrived at our house, she and I left for Los Angeles for the big announcement of who would be on *Dancing with the Stars* during its fourteenth season. Peta and I were on the same plane—but the producers told us we couldn't talk to each other. They didn't want anyone to know in advance that I was to be a contestant. She was with her boyfriend, and I was sitting behind her. I sat in my seat and didn't say a word to her. We passed notes to each other.

"I can't believe we can't talk to each other," she wrote.

"I know," I wrote back.

The next day, we arrived in Los Angeles at the studios of ABC, the host of *Dancing with the Stars,* for our introduction to the public. I was starstruck the first day. I was starstruck the whole time. As a Packer I had met numerous celebrities, but being on *Dancing with the Stars* gave me the opportunity to spend significant time with a group of celebrities I had come to admire during my life. I got to see them as real people, another part of the experience that I very much enjoyed.

One of the first celebrity contestants I saw was Maria Menounos, the host of the TV magazine show *Extra*.

"How are you doing, Mr. Driver?" she said. "I want you to know, I'm a Patriots fan."

"We're starting this already?" I said. "You're competing on the show, but I'm going to win. I'll bet you my Packers are going to beat your Patriots."

I met the cast members, the dancers, and the new contestants. Among them were Jaleel White, who as a teenager played the geeky Steve Urkel ("Did I do thaaaaaat?"). Jaleel said he was a big Packers fan.

I met Sherri Shepherd, a panelist on *The View*. She didn't know who I was, but I knew who she was. I was thrilled to meet music legend Gladys Knight.

"You're so cute," she cooed.

I melted.

I couldn't believe I was getting to meet Gladys Knight, even without the Pips.

I saw an actor I recognized.

"Hey, you're Roy from *The Five Heartbeats*," I said. "You were the one getting dumped over the balcony!"

He laughed.

"I'm Roy Fegan," he said. "My son Roshon is going to be a contestant."

Roshon Fegan is an actor on the popular Disney show *Shake It Up*, which my kids watch on TV. I was sure Cristian and Christina would be impressed that I had met him.

Then I was introduced to Gavin DeGraw.

Who is Gavin DeGraw? I wondered. I'd heard that name before. *What does he do?*

By a great coincidence the song "Sweeter" happened to come on the radio while DeGraw and I were in the makeup room.

"You like that song?" he asked.

"Yeah, man. It comes on the radio every time I'm in Dallas. Who sings that song?"

"Gavin DeGraw," he said.

"*You're* Gavin DeGraw? Man, I love that song. *You're* Gavin Degraw?"

I couldn't believe he was the one who sang it . . . until he started singing it for me. I went out and bought his CD the next day.

They told us that William Levy, a Latino actor, would not be at the introductions. They showed his picture on the jumbotron.

"Uh oh," I said. His dance partner was the talented Cheryl Burke, who had been on the show since the beginning and had won twice in a row with Drew Lachey and Emmitt Smith as her partners. I knew right away William and Cheryl were going to be very good. Then I met Jack Wagner. He starred for years in the soap operas *The Bold and the Beautiful* and *General Hospital*.

"My mom and my wife watch you all the time," I said to him.

I couldn't believe all the stars I was meeting in one place. I was sitting there thinking, *That's Melissa Gilbert from* Little House on the Prairie*!* I couldn't help but reminisce about all these people and these shows that we all grew up watching.

For me the one celebrity who stood out more than anybody was Martina Navratilova, the tennis legend.

"Martina, I love your story," I told her. "You were the first athlete to come out and announce that you were a lesbian. Awesome. You're great! That doesn't bother me at all.

"I'd love to go to a tennis match with you," I said.

"I'd love for you to come," she said.

I was in the same studio with these people for three and a half months. I couldn't wait to talk to them and get to know them better. We all felt we had a bond—every single person on the show felt that way. That was an amazing experience. We became like brothers and sisters.

I also got to know all the professional dancers. I already knew who they were from years of watching the show. We all became real close as the show went on. We started exchanging phone numbers. I never would have thought I could call Gladys Knight at home on the phone. Not in a million years did I ever think I would be able to just call her up and talk to her or that I could call Gavin DeGraw while he was performing in Milwaukee at Summerfest. I was supposed to be there, but I had to go back to Dallas from Los Angeles, so I wasn't in Wisconsin. Right before Gavin went onstage, he texted me and said to call him on his cellphone in about twenty minutes. He was onstage when I called him.

"Hold on," he told the crowd, "hold on, I have to answer this." And he said, 'Wisconsin, guess what? I have on the phone here my good buddy from *Dancing with the Stars*, Donald Driver!"

I yelled into his phone for all to hear, "Milwaukee, show

my boy some love!" The crowd just went nuts. I could hear the screaming and yelling. Even now, it still shocks me that I can pick up the phone and call Melissa Gilbert and say, "Hey, sweetheart, how's it going?"

Then there were the other celebrities I've met from being on the show. I met Academy Award winner and movie star Marlee Matlin. Her son is a big fan of mine. She and I text each other all the time. I also text with talk show host Ricki Lake. I would have never met all of these people had I not gone on the show.

ABC made *Dancing with the Stars* a first-class production. The contestants were treated fabulously.

I was in great shape to do this. I had gotten down to 2 percent body fat, the lowest I've ever been. People say that's unhealthy. Part of that is my metabolism.

Once I arrived in Los Angeles, I could hear from our phone conversations how unhappy Tina was. She was lonely. On the phone she would cry. I needed for her to come to Los Angeles to be with me so she could see that I wasn't doing anything wrong. Sometimes your fears are far worse than the reality, and she was so unhappy, I was finally able to convince her to bring the kids with her to Hollywood.

"That way we can be together as a family," I told her. "That way you can come to rehearsals and see that nothing's going on."

After ten days she and the kids flew to Los Angeles to be with me.

I'd awake early and do my workout for football, and then Peta and I would practice dancing all day. At night, when it was nice and cool, Tina and I would go jogging along Wilshire Boulevard. We would take off from our apartment and just run. I reassured Tina that this was a job, that nothing was going on, that she was the most important person in my life, and after a while she warmed up to Peta. She got to know her, and they became buddies. We all would double date. Cris and Christina would call her "Aunt Peta." They would go see her in her trailer.

As for the actual dancing and competing: Did you see the smile on my face the whole time? Well there you go. The work was grueling. I would practice dancing in a studio for hours, but the satisfaction I got from my improvement made it all worthwhile.

The challenge of the competition was great, and Peta quickly saw that if we were to have any chance of winning, I would have to control some of my macho tendencies. As a proud male who didn't want to be thought of as feminine, I wanted to act macho. I didn't want to get up there and shake my butt and move around. When the coaches and judges told me I had to move and sway my hips or my arms a certain way, initially I refused.

"That looks too feminine to me," I would say. "A tough guy doesn't do that!"

"You're not supposed to be tough," I was told by the coaches. "You're supposed to have fun. This is all about having fun."

From the beginning I learned I had to stop judging myself and just let go.

"Relax," Peta would say. "Quit being so tight-ass. Shake your body a little, move your hips. I know you can move—

you're black. I can't believe my partner is the only black man who can't move."

She would not let up until I started to do things her way.

"You can dance," she would say. "I've seen it. You can shake it."

She would say things like "I want you to 'give it' to Carrie Ann Inaba," one of the show's judges. "When you get down, I want you to roll your whole body, roll your hips, and you better be looking straight at Carrie Ann in our first cha-cha. I want you to make Carrie Ann say, 'Oooh yes!'"

"Okay," I said, not meaning it.

I was thinking, *I'm so out of my league.*

"Judge Len Goodman is all about technique," Peta explained. "He wants things perfect." She said the other judge, Bruno Tonioli, just wanted me to take my clothes off for him.

"If you take your clothes off for Bruno, you've got him," she said.

"Okay," I said, not meaning it.

I was thinking, *I'm so out of my league.*

In time I learned to go with the flow, and I ended up having so much fun as a male figure on that show. Every other man on that show would tell you the same thing, that they loved it, and you're talking about some of the most popular men in the world.

ANOTHER THING THAT I really liked about dancing on the show was becoming someone else onstage. They kept trying to bring my football career to the show. They would have me say promotional stuff like "It took Donald Driver thirteen years to win the Super Bowl, but he will only get one chance to win the Mirror Ball." I would roll my eyes. I began to realize that football was not my entire identity. I began to think of myself more as an entertainer.

Judge Bruno Tonioli made the statement "You should be in show business." He said he liked the way I expressed myself in my face. I would watch Mark Ballas, one of the professional dancers on the show, do that. I stole most of my shtick from Mark. He was always entertaining. He was always expressing himself. In my quick step, I borrowed one of his expressions. I saw how you get into character. I would go from being serious to fun to getting back into character.

Of course, part of dancing is being sexy.

Judge Carrie Ann declared that she wanted me to be sexy.

Okay, I wondered, *how sexy do you want me to be?*

"I want you to"—and let me paraphrase here—"have sex with Peta with your eyes," she said.

"How do you do that?" I asked.

"It's what dancers do," she said. "When you do the Argentine tango, I want you to make love to Peta on the floor. I want you to make everyone watching think, *That's hot.*"

In other words your dancing has to have a little sizzle with it.

Cheryl Burke and Kym Johnson would say about me, "Oh, he's so cute." Or "He's a handsome guy. Oh my God, look at him." One time Sherri Shepherd said, "I am in love with Donald Driver! Look at this man! Kunta Kinte don't have nothin' on him!"

The whole thing was a huge ego trip. It was also part of show business. I had all these famous people saying they were attracted to me when none of it meant a thing to me. A lot of it was hype for the show. In interviews Peta would say, "He's a good-looking man. He has all those muscles. Look at him. I'm going to work with this. That's not a bad-looking body up underneath all these clothes."

I was fine with all of it. Peta is a small woman, but she isn't the featherweight that people think she is. I had to pick her up, and she was a load. I could tease her about that, part of our brother-sister bond and relationship. I have video of the two of us playing around in practice, hitting each other, kicking each other, when we were supposed to be doing the *pasodoble*—a lively style of dance modeled after the sound, drama, and movement of the Spanish bullfight.

She kicked me for real in my stomach.

"You're just like my little brother who I used to beat up," she said.

I thought Peta was cool. She was beautiful, but I was not attracted to her. But as Carrie Ann was quick to remind me, if the judges and the public didn't think I was attracted to Peta while we were dancing, we weren't going to win. When I did the waltz, I was sexy as hell, and we scored very well. When I did the cha-cha, I took off my vest and threw it to Carrie Ann, giving Bruno just what he wanted. I danced bare-chested, showing off my muscles and my tattoos, and he was smitten.

To win I would have to be even sexier when I did the Argentine tango in the final show.

After nine whirlwind weeks of practicing long hours and

dancing for the nation to see, Peta and I were still alive. Martina Navratolova had been the first to be eliminated. Jack Wagner lost next. On consecutive weeks Sherri Shepherd, Gavin DeGraw, Jaleel White, and Roshon Fegan bit the dust.

Melissa Gilbert was next to go, followed by Maria Menounos.

For the final show, on May 22, 2012, three couples remained. William Levy and Cheryl Burke was one couple. Levy, who was born in Cuba, was a star on Mexican television. Kids knew him most from being Jennifer Lopez's love interest in her music video "I'm Into You." He certainly had his fans.

My other competition was Katherine Jenkins, a singer of classical music, who was paired with the very talented dancer Mark Ballas. I knew the competition would be fierce. Winning required getting the most points from the three judges, but half the score came from the public voting in a national election. I liked my chances. William Levy and Katherine Jenkins were unknowns when they entered the competition, but their charm, charisma, and dancing ability brought them to the attention of the entire country.

Who did I have rooting for me? Only the entire Green Bay Packers fandom and the entire state of Wisconsin.

To win, both Peta and I admitted we had to work on becoming the passionate couple the judges and the public were expecting. It was a matter now of learning to act, learning to become a character in a play, only this play was based on reality.

We were working on the tango, and I was messing up deliberately just for the hell of it. I then yelled at her to get her feet right. I was after her constantly, relentlessly criticizing her. Of course she had no idea why I was doing this, and she just looked at me puzzled.

"Leave the building," I ordered her. "We're not going to win. I should get another partner." I then pulled her close.

"I wish I had Cheryl as my partner," I said. "This sucks. I can't do this."

All of this was filmed on camera, of course. I was acting.

When her eyes started to get watery, I couldn't take it any longer.

"Peta," I said. "They told me to stir up some drama."

She hugged me but also said, "I could kill you right now."

For the final performance Carrie Ann coached me on how to hug and embrace Peta.

"I'll show you how," she said.

She wrapped her arms around me, seductively, breathing in my ear.

"How does that feel?" she asked.

"Like sexual harassment," I said.

In the finale we had to perform two dances, one the Argentine tango, the other a freestyle performance of our own choosing.

The first time I did the Argentine tango in front of Carrie Ann, who had been advising us, her reaction was that I was holding back my emotions so much that I didn't have a chance to win.

"The tango is a dance of love," Carrie Ann said, "and you aren't showing the love."

Carrie Ann knew her stuff. She said to me, "All the other women in the building probably think, "Oh my God, they've got something going on,' but I could see you were looking at Peta like she's your sister. You have to do it again, but this time you have to find the passion."

There never was that attraction between me and Peta, but at the same time we knew we needed for it to look that way when we performed our last Argentine tango. There had to be that sexual tension between us. In certain dances, especially Latin dances, sexiness and sex appeal are what it's all about. But up until this point I could only go so far.

"Why?" Carrie Ann asked me.

"Because I never want to make my wife feel uncomfortable," I said.

"I respect that," she said. "Not too many men come on the show and say that."

She suggested I bring Tina in to practice with us and that I picture Tina's face when I was looking at Peta.

"That way," she said, "you will make love to Tina by making love to Peta—but just by dancing."

I talked to Tina about it, explaining to her the importance of my looking like I was Peta's lover. Tina had been coming to rehearsals and came to understand what was needed. She told me to go ahead. Her permission was wholehearted. Tina is a remarkable woman.

As Peta and I went out onto the stage on that final night to dance the Argentine tango, I said, "All right, Peta! You're in trouble."

I winked at the judges. I let go and became that sexy Latin lover Carrie Ann wanted me to be.

If I want to win, I told myself, *I'm going to have to do this.*

I had that smoldering look in my eyes. I seduced Peta with everything I had while we danced, and every line, every move, turned out perfectly. Peta and I were connected. We had that longing look in our eyes.

Dancing the Argentine tango, we just rocked the house being silly and having fun.

The final dance was a freestyle number. William Levy went first, and he and his partner did a Latin dance, and he scored 10, 10, and got a 9 from Len Goodman, who complained that Levy was doing the expected. Katherine went next. She opened up by singing—she sings beautifully—and she and her partner really nailed it, scoring a perfect 30.

Now it was our turn. We needed to be perfect to keep up. I chose to do something completely unexpected. We would dance to a country-and-western song, and we'd do a little hip-hop dancing at the end. We wore green and yellow costumes, harking back to my Green Bay Packers roots.

Peta and I just went out and had as much fun as we could. We swayed and shimmied and shook and boogied, and when we were done, I thought the roof was going to come off the building.

Carrie Ann said it was her favorite dance of the night and gave us a 10. Len finally gave us a 10, and so did Bruno. It was one of the closest finals ever. It would all come down to the voting public. How many cheeseheads would call 1-800-868-3403 and vote for us? I had high hopes.

The three finalists sat on the stage to await the announcement of who won. First Tom Bergeron announced the third-place finisher.

"In third place with the judges votes and the fan voting, the third place goes to"—we waited and waited and waited—"William Levy and Cheryl Burke."

We gave them a hug and wished them well. Now only two were left.

Bergeron announced, "When we come back, one of them will leave with the trophy." My heart was racing.

Before the show I had told the producers that if we won I wanted Tina to bring my baby daughter Charity onto the stage. As Katherine Jenkins, Mark Ballas, Peta, and I were coming down to where they were going to make the final announcement, I looked to my right where Tina was, and I thought I could see Charity.

"Peta," I said to her, "do you remember when I told you I wanted Charity here if we won?"

"Yes," she said.

"Look to your right and tell me if you see Charity. If she's there, we've won."

"I'm not going to look," she said. "What if she's not there?"

"Then we've lost."

We sat there, our eyes straight ahead.

After the commercial Tom Bergeron said, "We will now reveal the winner. The winner of *Dancing with the Stars* in its fourteenth season"—the pause was so long it seemed like it was all day, even though it was only perhaps thirty seconds—"Donald and Peta."

I jumped up and started running. I fell to the floor and started rolling around. I came back and hugged Peta. It was like I had just won the Super Bowl all over again.

"How does it feel?" Bergeron asked me.

"Amazing," I said. "Awesome."

And that was how I felt.

Peta and I held up the beautiful Mirror Bowl as Tina, Charity, Christina, and Cristian rushed onto the stage to congratulate us. As the cameras panned the celebration I held Charity in my arms and I kissed and hugged Tina. I then hugged the other contestants.

It was one of the most amazing moments I have ever experienced.

OTHER THAN THE millions of cheeseheads, before I performed on *Dancing with the Stars* no one knew who Donald Driver was. But I couldn't help but think how many Green Bay Packers fans watched the show because of me. And voted for me. I'm sure that Peta and I won the contest because of them. And because Peta and I can dance.

I had told Peta when I first met her, "Get ready, because all we have to do is dance well. If we do, the Packers fans are going to keep us in the competition."

"There's no way," she said.

She had no idea.

"You don't know Packer Nation," I said. "Packer Nation is huge."

She looked at me as if to say, *Yeah, right.*

She didn't know football at all.

But it was a turning point for me. It told me how much I meant to the fans. They supported me throughout the show, and because of them I had 33 percent more votes than any other contestant.

It was a great experience. I'd have to say it was one of the best experiences of my life. I tell people that winning the Mirror Bowl and the *Dancing with the Stars* championship was as satisfying as winning the Super Bowl.

The show is a lot more than dancing. The viewers have to know the hard work the contestants put into it. Packers fans *knew* what I put into it. They saw all the work. And I've had more men tell me they've taken up dancing with their wives, or are taking dance lessons because of my being on the show. That's *big* for me. It's a great compliment. I was able to get these men out of being tough guys and off to a party where they can dance with their wives.

Tina and I dance at home now. We'll dance, and I'll be counting the steps, and she'll say, "Babe, we need some work."

But she's having fun. She goes back on the Internet and watches the dances to learn to do certain moves.

"Can we kick our feet like that? We'll have to figure out how we can put that into our routine."

Because of *Dancing with the Stars*, the world now knows who I am. Yes, they know I played football and they know I'm a dance champion, but more important, they now know this guy is a good guy. He's a good Christian man. He believes. He loves his family dearly. He loves his kids. People saw all of that on the show, and now I have a bigger fan base than ever.

I don't know what the future holds for me, but because of *Dancing with the Stars* my world has opened for me. Now I'm not too shy to say, "I want to be in a movie." Or to say,

"I can work for *Good Morning America*." Before I went on the show, I would have been too fearful. Now I have the confidence to be a correspondent for a news show, where I can report important stories about sports.

Thanks to *Dancing with the Stars,* the world is my oyster.

CHAPTER 14

TIME
TO SAY
GOODBYE

After appearing on *Dancing with the Stars*, I was the featured guest on *Ellen*, with Ellen DeGeneres. I wasn't happy she said she was a fan of the New Orleans Saints, but I certainly was glad to hear she also rooted for the Packers. Peta and I were guests on *Jimmy Kimmel Live*. Jimmy had predicted the first week that Peta and I would win, and I was very happy to congratulate him for his clairvoyance. I was a guest with Kelly Ripa. I wonder if I hadn't gone back and played football for one more year that people would be watching the show *Kelly and Donald*. A year later I was a cohost with Katie Couric, appearing as the first cohost she had for *Katie*. It was a wedding special, and I talked about how I surprised Betina on our tenth anniversary with a party for our closest one hundred friends.

I also returned to my life as a football player. I was thirty-seven years old, hoping I could continue to be productive in a game that trumpeted the young and denigrated and put to pasture the old. I was at a Packers event for kids with diabetes in the off-season when a television reporter asked me, "If you return to the Packers, would you be willing to take a pay cut?"

I liked to be politically correct in front of the media, so my answer was, "I would be happy to. I'd do anything for the organization. That's what I'm all about."

What else could I say? Had I said "No," I would have

been accused of being selfish, not a team player, that all I wanted was the money.

Sometimes as an athlete you just can't win.

In this case that was certainly true, because not long after I went on *Dancing with the Stars* in May of 2012, Packers general manager Ted Thompson announced that if I wanted to continue as a Packer, I would have to sign a new deal with them. My old contract called for me to be paid $5 million for 2012, and they didn't want to pay me close to that much.

Every time I got ready to negotiate a contract, I always went to Ted first and told him exactly what I was looking for. He would always tell me the same story: "Donald, I'm not going to get into numbers with you, but we'll look at it."

"Tell me," I'd plead with him. "What are we looking at?"

"Donald," he would say every time, "I'll talk to your agent."

The same line he gave to the media about salaries he would give to me. He put up that wall. Meanwhile while we talked he'd sit there with a pen and a yellow pad and take notes while I was talking. I would be walking out, and Ted would still be writing.

"Are we still friends?" Ted would ask as I was leaving. The next day we'd joke about it.

After this negotiation in which the Packers didn't give me much wiggle room, I wasn't laughing. In the end I signed a new deal for far less money—a fifty percent pay cut—because I wanted to play for the Packers and because at the end of the day the money wasn't the most important thing.

I was very disappointed because when I signed my contract only two years earlier, the Packers insisted I bring my entire family to the signing, and during the ceremony Thompson told the press, "Congratulations, Donald. You will retire as a Packer."

Contracts at the end of a career sometimes are not only for what you can do on the field but also what you have done for the organization over your entire career. A year later, they pulled the rug out from under me, cancelling my contract and forcing me to take a significant pay cut if I wanted to stay with the team.

"Or else," Packers GM Ted Thompson told my agent, "we're going to let Donald go."

After so many years of my loyalty, this was very difficult to accept.

When we were negotiating my new contract I refused to allow them to put in an incentive clause, because it would have been too easy for them to just sit me on the sidelines in order to save money. In the end I signed for half of the original salary. They also cut my signing bonus.

I understand that sports is also a business, but it hurt me as it had hurt Brett Favre before me. And when you're slapped around like that, you begin to question whether you want to be around here anymore.

I was sure there were teams that would have loved to have had me had I refused the pay cut and became a free agent. Joe Philbin took the head coaching job with the Miami Dolphins, a team that didn't have top receivers. Reggie McKenzie went to Oakland to become their general manager. He was once our director of player personnel and he knew what I could do. Jimmy Robinson, my former position coach, was in Dallas with the Cowboys.

In the end I came back to Green Bay for another season because of my teammates and because of the fans. They had supported me with *Dancing with the Stars*. They had supported me when I held my charity softball game in June in Appleton. They had voted me as one of the most popular players in the NFL along with Peyton Manning, Brian Urlacker, Robert Griffin III, and Drew Brees. If I had left the Packers, I would have sorely disappointed them. Worse, I would have been disloyal to them.

Tina also would have been unhappy. She loves Green Bay. She told me, "You love Green Bay. Let's not leave on a bitter note. Sign the new deal. At the end of the day we don't need the money that badly."

It hurt but you move on. And of course, it was still a lot of money.

I signed with Green Bay and put the rancor and hurt feelings behind me.

In 2012, my fourteenth year with the Packers in what turned out to be my swan song, there wasn't much to write home about as I caught 8 passes for 77 yards and two touchdowns.

In the second game of the season against the Chicago Bears, I caught a 26-yard pass from Aaron for a touchdown. Even so, I could see I was spending much of my time on the bench as Coach McCarthy was going with the younger receivers, Randall Cobb, James Jones, Jordy Nelson, and Greg Jennings.

I wasn't used much against Seattle, New Orleans, and Indianapolis, and before the next game, which was scheduled for my hometown of Houston, Coach McCarthy called me into his office.

"Donald," he said, "I'm looking down the road, and in a couple weeks you may not dress for the game. We're not sure how it's going to work as far as who's up, who's down, who's injured, and who's healthy."

Wow, was what I thought. *I haven't been playing much, but I had no idea I was no longer in their plans.*

I was stunned, and more than a little hurt.

I continued to play sparingly. In the eighth game of the season against Jacksonville I made a catch, and when I was tackled I put my hand out to brace myself. My thumb must have hit the ground first, because when I caught the next pass, I couldn't get a grip on the ball. I switched the ball to my other hand, and I stepped out of bounds. Later in the game I caught a touchdown pass, but after the game I asked our doctor to take a look at the hand. I didn't want to take my glove off. When I removed it, my thumb was fat, the swelling obvious. The next day it was worse. It turned out I had a torn ligament and a broken bone.

It didn't stop me from playing. I wore a cast on it during the week, and I took it off game days. In the next game against Arizona I dropped a pass, and another pass bounced off my chest because I just couldn't grip the ball.

I had a cortisone shot in the thumb before the Detroit game, and I was able to catch a pass over the middle, but as the season went along the thumb never got any better. For week 13 against the Minnesota Vikings, the Packers chose not to dress me for the game. It was only the second time I was inactive since 2007.

The rumor mill began saying that I was unhappy with Aaron Rodgers, but that wasn't at all true. As long as we won games, I never cared who got the ball. My attitude always was, *If I don't get any catches, and we win, great.* I cared about my records, but by this time I had gotten my records.

I am very proud of my numbers. I finished my career with 743 catches for 10,137 yards, both Green Bay Packers career records. Only eighteen receivers in NFL history have more than 700 catches and over 10,000 yards.

I can remember as I was getting close to breaking Sterling Sharpe's career reception record of 595, he would call me on the phone and jokingly say to me, "I'm going to call Aaron and make sure he doesn't throw the ball to you this week so you won't break my record."

We would laugh. And then in October of 2009 against the Detroit Lions, I caught number 596, and after the game Sterling called to congratulate me. Normally people don't want their records broken and become resentful, but Sterling was a real gentleman, a class guy.

I remember catching the ball around the ten-yard line. I could see the end zone. Sterling had told me, "When you break the record, make sure you score a touchdown," but when I got hit by three Lion defenders, I knew that wasn't going to happen. I got up, and after the record was announced, I held up the ball and blew a kiss to the crowd.

This is amazing, I thought. *The street kid from the slums of Houston is now the leader in receptions in Green Bay Packers history.*

I am also the Packers leader in receiving yards. I went

back to look in the record book. After me are some Hall of Fame-worthy receivers, James Lofton with 9,656 yards, Sterling Sharpe with 8,134 yards, the legendary Don Hutson with 7,991 yards, and Vince Lombardi's favorite, Boyd Dowler with 6,918 yards.

How did I surpass those guys? I marveled.

God has truly blessed me.

I broke James Lofton's career yards record on September 18, 2011, against the Carolina Panthers. I was honored when James called me afterward to congratulate me.

"You deserve everything," he said magnanimously. James also wore number 80, and he generously said to me, "You have made the number special." No, James, *you* made the number famous. If I did the number proud it was only to give it more glory.

I finished my career with 61 touchdown receptions, third in Packers history to Don Hutson with 99 and Shannon Sharpe with 65. I'm first in Packers history to make receptions in 133 games in a row, and I'm second in Packers history in games played with 205. Only Brett Favre, with 255, has more. I'm also second in Packers history with 10,354 yards from the line of scrimmage behind Ahman Green with 11,048.

To be ranked with players like these gives me goose bumps just to think about it. I cherish my fourteen years with the Packers and what we have accomplished, a Super Bowl win, five division titles, a new NFL record in team offense, and only two losing seasons. To be part of all of that has been very special. In fact, it blows my mind.

At the same time I knew I was faced with a choice:

I knew I was no longer in Coach McCarthy's plans, and so I could do what Reggie White, Antonio Freeman, and Brett Favre did—leave the Packers to go play for another team. Or I could save the Packers and myself a lot of bad feelings and retire as a Packer.

As the season wound down I decided to discuss what to do with my wife and kids.

"I think the organization is moving in another direction," I told her. "They want to go with the young players."

"If you want to go someplace else and play," Tina said, "I'm fine with that. Wherever you go, the kids and I will be right there with you."

I asked her, "How would you feel if I decided not to play any more football? How would you feel if I was home all the time, just seeing me here, hugging you, right up under your nose all day long?"

She smiled.

"I'd love it," she said.

I asked my nine-year-old son, Cristian.

"Dad," he said with a maturity beyond his years, "you've done everything you wanted to do. You're the all-time Packers leading receiver. You have a Super Bowl ring. We have a miracle [Charity, our two-year-old]. I don't think you have to prove anything else."

When I asked my little daughter, Christina, she burst out crying.

"I think Daddy knows why," I said.

Throughout her young life, all the time she would ask me, "Daddy, why do you have to go?"

I'd tell her, "Daddy has a job playing football. Dad has to go to practice. Dad has to go to a game. Dad has to do this or that."

Now Daddy would be home to be at all her activities.

I even asked little Charity.

She nodded her head yes, and it made me laugh. As a family we decided it was time for me to walk away from the game, even though I still had the ability to play at a high level.

After our family meeting, I made my decision that I would retire. Before the end of the 2012 season I told my teammates. In the locker room I let it be known, "Hey, this might be my last year." I wasn't saying it officially, but I wanted them to know.

Some of them said, "Drive, you can still play. Go somewhere else and play. You love the game so much. Play."

"It's not about me," I told them. "It's about my family. They want to be settled. It'll be great not to have to go back and forth between our homes in Dallas and Green Bay."

When I told Aaron, he gave me a look as if to ask, *Are you sure?*

I had played in Brett Favre's shadow, and he had passed the torch to me, and I told Aaron, "It's time for me to hang it up and let you be the face of the franchise like you're supposed to be.

"Let's go out with a bang and win another Super Bowl."

I then told the receiver corps. We were a big family.

"I love you guys," I told them. "It was great playing with you."

In the end the Packers didn't get into the Super Bowl,

though we came close. I was put on the inactive list for the wild-card playoff win over the Minnesota Vikings, and we finished out our season when we lost to the San Francisco 49ers the next week.

The next day I met with Coach McCarthy to discuss my future during my after-the-season exit interview.

"What are your plans?" he wanted to know. That in itself told me he wasn't going to bring me back. It was time to put up or shut up.

"I'm not going to put you through the stress and pain of trying to figure out where I'm going to go," I told him. "I'm going to make it easy on you guys as well as the fans, and I will retire as a Packer."

I had learned a lot over the course of my career. Earlier on, I had watched when Reggie White wanted to play one more year for Green Bay, but didn't get invited back. Ten years later it was Brett Favre, who had been tossed aside by the Packers and who had said to me, "Your time will come, too. And what decision are you going to make?"

I decided to walk away as a member of the Green and Gold. The Packers were my first team, and they would be my only team.

I told general manager Ted Thompson and team CEO Mark Murphy the same thing. I also told Mark that I wanted to do something special for the fans. He said he'd agree to whatever I wanted to do.

In early February of 2013 I was in New Orleans before the Super Bowl game between San Francisco and Baltimore. My first interview was on ESPN's *Mike and Mike in the Morning,* and it was on that show that I officially announced my retirement. I was able to publicly invite the Packers fans to join me on February 6 for a news conference/going away ceremony at Lambeau Field. I wanted to thank the fans personally. The Packers gave away two thousand tickets to fans for the event. They were gone in fifteen minutes. I couldn't believe it. A couple of fans even stayed up all night in the freezing cold to get tickets.

That day was a love-fest between the Packers fans and me. As I stood in the atrium of Lambeau Field, the fans hanging over the balcony above, fans all around me, I couldn't help breaking into tears. Tina cried as well.

"I was the same guy who walked in in 1999," I told the crowd, "and I'm the same guy who walks out in 2013. People say that success sometimes changes who you are—success has not changed me. I'm the same skinny little kid who walked in in 1999. I'll be the same skinny kid—well, grown man—who walks out in 2013. Nothing changes for me. I'm the same person and never will change."

Tears ran down my face as I spoke those words. At that moment I felt my career was over, that I was done playing football. I was going to miss all those fans, millions and millions of them around the world. I was going to miss the 80,000 fans who filled Lambeau Field every Packers home game. I was going to miss running out of the tunnel to the roar of that crowd.

I was also going to miss Green Bay and its fans. When I arrived in Green Bay, I had no clue what to expect, but I didn't know the history behind this great franchise. When I started to study it I thought we had an owner. We don't. I found out the community owns the team. Millions of fans including myself,

Tina, and my three kids own stock. The Packers sold more shares as a way to pay for the renovation of the new stadium.

Every time I go somewhere and they tell me they own a share of the Packers, I smile because they are the ones writing the checks. That shows you how much love the fans have for the players.

I knew Green Bay was a small town, but I never realized how small. My first reaction was, *Is this all there is?* But as time went on I began to see how special this place is. I became a fan favorite. I've never been to an event where I didn't have thousands of fans supporting me. It tells you what the community means to you, and you mean to the community. That's why when I retired, I opened up my retirement to the fans, because it wasn't *my* retirement. It was *our* retirement.

Because of what I've done on and off the field, the fans will always be able to say, "Donald is our guy."

I was also going to really miss the guys in the locker room and everything else around the game, and what was special was that Tina and my children were there to experience it with me.

I will always have my memories, and I will always be grateful to all of you.

ACKNOWLEDGMENTS

I WANT TO thank God, and also thanks to my entire family, especially my mother for being the strong woman that you are; my father for making me the man that I am; my grandparents George and Betty Lofton for raising me in the Lord; and to Elzie and Stella Brock Jr. for helping me to believe that everything and anything is possible.

I would like to thank my siblings, Tamela, Moses aka Marvin Driver III, Trice aka Patricia, and Lil Sam, who I experienced life with. I want to thank my mother-in-law, Mrs. Inett Jackson, and my father-in-law, the late Walter Jackson, and my stepdad Sam Gray Jr, for taking us in and loving us. Thanks, too, to all my uncles and aunts.

Thanks to my high school coaches, Mike Truelove, Jimmy Duffer, and Boyce Honea; my college coach Cordell Jones; to Alicia Shields and to the entire Packers organization, including Bret Favre, Ron Wolf, Bob Harlan, Ray Rhodes, Mike Sherman, Mike McCarthy, Ray Sherman, James Franklin, Jimmy Robinson, and Edgar Bennett. My special thanks to Pleasant Hill Baptist Church, pastor Johnny White and Calvary Baptist Church, pastors Barker and Cummings.

I would like to thank my friend and agent Brian Lammi, the entire Lammi Sport Family team, cowriter Lori Nickel, and my writing partner Peter Golenbock. Also my thanks to my editor, Mary Choteborsky, of Crown Publishers, and all my business partners.

Lastly, to the BROS . . . You know who you are.

LOVE YOU ALL!!!!!!!!!!!!!!!!!!!!!!

DONALD DRIVER

INDEX